40 DAYS IN THE

WORD & SPIRIT

R.T. KENDALL

CHARISMA HOUSE

Most Charisma House Book Group products are available at special quantity discounts for bulk purchase for sales promotions, premiums, fund-raising, and educational needs. For details, call us at (407) 333-0600 or visit our website at www.charismahouse.com.

40 Days in the Word and Spirit by R. T. Kendall
Published by Charisma House
Charisma Media/Charisma House Book Group
600 Rinehart Road, Lake Mary, Florida 32746

Visit the author's website at www.rtkendallministries.com.

Library of Congress Cataloging-in-Publication Data:
An application to register this book for cataloging has been submitted to the Library of Congress.
International Standard Book Number: 978-1-63641-002-9
E-book ISBN: 978-1-64341-003-6

Portions of this book were previously published by Charisma House as *Word and Spirit*, ISBN 978-1-62999-649-3, copyright © 2019; and as *The Word and the Spirit* in the United Kingdom by Kingsway Publications, ISBN 0-85476-413-5, copyright © 1996, and in the United States by Charisma House, ISBN 0-88419-544-9, copyright © 1998.

21 22 23 24 25 — 9 8 7 6 5 4 3 2 1
Printed in the United States of America

CONTENTS

INTRODUCTION

I N THE THIRD chapter of Acts, Peter and John were on their way to the temple. There, a man who had been lame from birth sat at the temple gate. Day after day, he was carried to that exact position so he could beg for alms from passersby. On this day, however, Peter and John turned aside and spoke to the man. "And fixing his eyes on him, with John, Peter said, 'Look at us.' So he gave them his attention, expecting to receive something from them. Then Peter said, 'Silver and gold I do not have, but what I do have I give you: In the name of Jesus Christ of Nazareth, rise up and walk'" (Acts 3:4–6, NKJV). The man was completely healed, and the crowds were amazed. Seeing the crowd's response, Peter confronted them:

> Men of Israel, why do you marvel at this? Or why look so intently at us, as though by our own power or godliness we had made this man walk? The God of Abraham, Isaac, and Jacob, the God of our fathers, glorified His Servant Jesus, whom you delivered up and denied in the presence of Pilate, when he was determined to let Him go. But you denied the Holy One and the Just, and asked for a murderer to be granted to you, and killed the Prince of life, whom God raised from the dead, of which we are witnesses. And His name, through faith in His name, has made this man strong, whom you see and know. Yes, the

faith which comes through Him has given him this perfect soundness in the presence of you all.

—Acts 3:12–16, nkjv

This is a very important passage of Scripture, and it gets
more important to me every time I read it. It shows what is
possible when the Word and the Spirit come together at the
same time. All around the world, there has been a silent divorce
within the church between God's Word and His Spirit. And,
unfortunately, like an actual divorce, the children of God have
become divided along this line.

The message of those on the Word side is that we must get
back to the Bible, reformation teaching, expository teaching,
and "earnestly contend for the faith which was once delivered
unto the saints" (Jude 3, kjv). Until this happens, this camp
says, the honor of God's name will not be restored. What's
wrong with this emphasis? Nothing. It is exactly right.

On the Spirit side, the message is that we need to get back to
the Book of Acts where there were signs, wonders, and miracles. We need the gifts of the Spirit in operation and manifesta-
tions of God's power. Until that kind of power is restored to the
church, the honor of God's name will not be restored. What's
wrong with that emphasis? Nothing. It's exactly right.

But the day is coming when there will be a spontaneous
combustion as these two sides simultaneously reconnect. Then,
the honor of God's name will truly be restored. Then, there will
be preaching with such power that an outpouring of signs and
wonders will result as the centrality of the Gospel is shared.
That is what we see in this passage of Acts: the miraculous

healing power of God intertwined with the preaching of the truth of Jesus Christ—the Word and the Spirit, hand in hand.

We will see a reunification of God's Word and His Spirit. As Bobby Conner has prophesied, the fear of the Lord is returning to the church, just as in the days after Pentecost "fear came upon every soul: and many wonders and signs were done by the apostles" (Acts 2:43, KJV). It is our unique privilege and responsibility to prepare ourselves, as the body of Christ, to receive the complete and undiluted message of God's kingdom.

It is my prayer that as you read through this devotional, you would understand the cost of the silent divorce that has taken place and that you would begin to anticipate the new move of God that will remarry His Word and His Spirit. Let us treasure the infallible Word of God, and let us surrender completely to the workings of His Holy Spirit.

May God the Father, Son, and Holy Spirit bless you and keep you now and evermore. Amen.

THE SILENT DIVORCE

After they prayed, the place where they were meeting
was shaken. And they were all filled with the Holy
Spirit and spoke the word of God boldly.
—ACTS 4:31, NIV

I CANNOT THINK OF anything that would honor God more or threaten Satan more than the Word and the Spirit coming together simultaneously, as was demonstrated in the Book of Acts. As long as these two remain separated to any degree, it becomes easier for the devil to keep the church from making a significant impact on the world.

When I say there has been a silent divorce between the Word and the Spirit, I mean that with many people today it has been one or the other. Some are well acquainted with the Scriptures. They know their Bibles. They know their doctrine. They know their church history. They can detect heresy a mile away. I call these people Word people.

Meanwhile, others emphasize the power of the Holy Spirit, some being well acquainted with the raw power of God. They have experienced the infilling of the Holy Spirit. They have experienced His gifts. They have seen healings, even miracles.

And they can detect dead orthodoxy a mile away. I call these people Spirit people.

There is nothing wrong with either emphasis. Each is exactly right. Take, for an example, those of us who represent the Reformed tradition, as I do. We say, "We must earnestly contend for the faith once delivered unto the saints. We must recover our Reformation heritage. We must return to the God of Jonathan Edwards and Charles Spurgeon. We must be sound in doctrine."

Or take another example: those who come from a Pentecostal or Charismatic perspective. They say, "We must recover apostolic power. The need of the day is for a renewal of the gifts of the Spirit. Signs and wonders were seen in the Book of Acts; we too must see them. What is needed is a demonstration of power."

My message is this: the church generally will struggle on and on in its plea for God to restore the honor of His name until not one or the other but *both*—the Scriptures and the power of God, the Word and the Spirit—coalesce simultaneously.

We are living at a time when the fear of God is mostly absent in the church, speaking generally. The world is not afraid of us or threatened by us but instead thumbs its nose at us while we are in a deep sleep. There is no sense of outrage anymore over conditions in society.

The advance of evil throughout the world is now so swift that we have watched standards of morality and decency degenerate before our eyes without it bothering us as it once might have. Until the fear of God returns to the church, humanity's ways will go "from bad to worse" (2 Tim. 3:13). This is because the church, according to Jesus, is "the salt of the earth." But He also said that if the salt loses its taste, "it is no longer good for anything except to be thrown out and trampled under people's feet" (Matt. 5:13).

I'm sorry—I wish it were not so, but this is precisely what the church is like in many parts of the world as I write these lines. The only thing that will bring the fear of God back to the church—aside from the pure Gospel of Christ—is for the Word of God and the Holy Spirit to come together in equal measure.

One of my contributions at the first Word and Spirit Conference in 1992 was not an expository sermon but rather a statement. It is called "Isaac." The apostle Paul gave an allegory about Hagar and Ishmael and Sarah and Isaac. (See Galatians 4:21–23.) Paul did this in the context of showing the purpose and place of the Law. What I have done with the original account is to apply it prophetically to our day.

I believe that ancient history is repeating itself. In the same way that Abraham sincerely thought Ishmael was the promised son, many have believed the current Pentecostal-Charismatic movement is *the* ultimate revival that God promised before the second coming. I question this. It is my view that a move of the Spirit far greater than any movement in church history— namely, "Isaac"—is coming. It will be a work of God more significant than anything heretofore seen, even in proportion to Isaac's greatness over Ishmael.

The church is on the brink of a post-Charismatic era of unprecedented glory. In my opinion it is the *same* as the midnight cry that we read about in the parable of the ten virgins (Matt. 25:1–13). It is when the Word and the Spirit come together as seen in the Book of Acts. Smith Wigglesworth (1859–1947) said much the same thing.

I believe "Isaac" will arrive suddenly without any further

notice when the church is in a deep, deep spiritual sleep—expecting nothing. This is precisely where we are now. The church generally being in deep sleep is the most accurate description of the church at the present time. This wake-up call can happen at any moment, and it is coming very soon.

The question is, Are we ready for it?

PERSONAL REFLECTION

Are you aware of the silent divorce that has happened between God's Word and His Spirit within the body of believers? Consider your own spiritual background. Which camp would your church, or the church you grew up in, lean toward?

_____

_____

_____

How does it feel to you to have the current Pentecostal-Charismatic movement referred to as "Ishmael"? What do you imagine an "Isaac" move of the Spirit would entail? How could you prepare your heart for that significant work of God on the earth?

_____

_____

_____

THE CONSCIOUS PRESENCE

For the kingdom realm of God comes with
power, not simply impressive words.
—1 CORINTHIANS 4:20, TPT

IT IS POSSIBLE to have the Word without the Spirit—that is, the Word without the conscious presence of the Holy Spirit. To understand what I mean by this, you must first understand that there is a difference between the *conscious* presence of the Spirit and the *unconscious* presence of the Spirit.

When Paul said, "Our gospel came to you not only in word, but also in power and in the Holy Spirit" (1 Thess. 1:5), he implied that one *could* preach the Word without power and without the Holy Spirit. He meant that the *conscious* presence of God was manifest in Thessalonica. He said virtually the same thing to the Corinthians: "My speech and my message were not in plausible words of wisdom, but in demonstration of the Spirit and of power" (1 Cor. 2:4).

In both instances, Paul could testify to the *conscious* presence of the Spirit. Likewise, in both cases, Paul implies that he might have spoken in word only. But he didn't—at least not in those instances. The conscious presence of the Holy Spirit accompanied his preaching with power. He knew this was essential to effective preaching.

For this reason, he asked the Ephesians to pray for him that he be given "words" to proclaim the Gospel "boldly" (Eph. 6:19). *Words* comes from the Greek *logos*, which we will examine in more detail below. *Boldly* comes from *parrēsia*, which means "boldness" or "freedom in speaking."[1] It is what Peter had when he preached on the day of Pentecost (Acts 2:14–40). It was what Paul wanted the Ephesians to ask for in prayer. I am sure God answered their prayer, but if such freedom, boldness, or utterance came inevitably every time Paul stood up to preach, he would not have asked the Ephesians to pray for him as he did. He was not merely displaying humility by asking for their prayers; he knew that without the power of the Spirit giving him utterance and boldness, his efforts would be far less effective.

There is a sense in which the Word and Spirit are inseparable but not *consciously* inseparable. If you say that the Word and the Spirit are unconsciously inseparable, I would agree. First of all, we would not have the Old and New Testaments without the Spirit. The Holy Spirit wrote the Bible, as we will see in more detail later. However, it does not follow that the Spirit will always apply the Word. Sometimes the Holy Spirit applies the Word and sometimes, owing to His sovereign prerogative, He doesn't. A printed word on a billboard can quote a scripture.

You see this in Bible Belt states in America, especially in Tennessee, where we live at the moment. Millions—saved and lost—see these scriptures as they drive down a highway. John 3:16 is sometimes quoted: "For God so loved the world, that he gave his only begotten Son, that whosoever believeth in him should not perish, but have everlasting life" (KJV). If the Word and the Spirit were inseparable, then why do not all lost people get saved when they read this? The answer is that the Spirit does not always *apply* the Word. Why not? Because God is sovereign.

In other words, there are times when God chooses to withhold His conscious presence. Isaiah discovered a truth we all face sooner or later: "Truly, you are a God who hides himself, O God of Israel, the Savior" (Isa. 45:15). That said, there will be those who foolishly choose *not* to take oil in their lamps as we all await the coming of the Bridegroom (Matt. 25:3). The lamp is a symbol of the Word: "Your word is a lamp to my feet and a light to my path" (Ps. 119:105). The oil is a symbol of the Holy Spirit. When Samuel poured the oil upon David, "the Spirit of the LORD rushed upon David from that day forward" (1 Sam. 16:13).

Jonathan Edwards (1703–1758) preached "Sinners in the Hands of an Angry God" on July 8, 1741, in Enfield, Connecticut. As great conviction seized his hearers, people were seen holding on to tree trunks to keep from sliding into Hell. But Edwards had preached the same sermon in Northampton, Massachusetts, and there was no apparent effect whatever.

One would hope for unusual power every time one preaches. However, even the great apostle Paul was acutely aware that he might speak to people without the conscious enablement of the Spirit. This is why he prayed to be given *words*—utterance, unusual ability to think and preach when the Holy Spirit not only pours thoughts into one's mind but also grants boldness for which there is no natural explanation. Merely to preach doctrine, however accurate that teaching might be, would not be enough. My mentor, Dr. Martyn Lloyd-Jones, used to slap the wrists of those "sound" preachers who were "perfectly orthodox but perfectly useless."[2]

In a word, we need not only the Scriptures but also the power of God. It is the conscious power of God that (surely) every preacher wants.

Personal Reflection

Have you ever spoken something that was true but that you could tell was not filled with the Spirit? How did your words affect those that heard them? How did you feel? Consider the alternative: Have you ever found yourself speaking something simple that had a surprisingly profound impact on others? What was the difference?

_____

_____

_____

Have you ever read a familiar passage of Scripture only to have the words come to life in a new way? How do you experience the conscious presence of the Spirit?

_____

_____

_____

GOD'S WORD

For the word of God is living and powerful, and sharper
than any two-edged sword, piercing even to the division
of soul and spirit, and of joints and marrow, and is a
discerner of the thoughts and intents of the heart.
—HEBREWS 4:12, NKJV

IT IS SADLY true today that most Christians—whether liberal, Evangelical, or Charismatic—*do not know their Bibles*. It does not help that less and less expository preaching exists in the church today throughout the world. Topical or motivational preaching has largely dominated the airwaves in our day. Not that there is anything wrong with topical or motivational preaching. The best of God's servants have done it and still do. But a key component of expository preaching is a high view of Scripture. One is hardly motivated to preach chapter by chapter—not to mention verse by verse—if he or she does not believe the Holy Spirit inspires every word.

God used people in writing the Bible, yes. Their personalities, style, cultural backgrounds, and theological presuppositions are apparent. But their words are still Spirit-breathed and infallible.

Peter said, "Whoever speaks, as one who speaks oracles of God" (1 Pet. 4:11). *Oracles* comes from *logia*—from *logos*, "word." The New International Version translates it "the very words of

God." The idea of oracle is that the Deity speaks through the person. Ideal preaching would be when God Himself owns our words so much that the hearers feel as if God Himself is confronting them.

Consider the preaching of Jesus: it was a case of being confronted by God Himself, for Jesus was (and is) God, and all His words mirrored the will of the Father (John 5:19). This is why His hearers were astonished; He spoke not as the scribes did but as one with authority (Matt. 7:28–29). Authority is what characterized Peter's preaching on the day of Pentecost. The scoffing that preceded Peter's sermon turned into people being "cut to the heart" and asking, "What shall we do?" (Acts 2:37).

Peter's sermon embodies what preaching was meant to be: the proclamation of the Word of God *through human personality*. A person's background, culture, accent, natural ability, and education—or lack of it—will often be apparent, even if the person speaks with great anointing and power. During the Cane Ridge Revival (1801) in Bourbon County, Kentucky, called America's Second Great Awakening by church historians, many uneducated preachers joined in exhorting simultaneously with a half dozen others who were preaching at a large camp meeting. Hundreds and hundreds were converted. Mockers who showed up to criticize got saved. Because many of these preachers were uneducated but effective, many were led to believe that education and training were not only unnecessary but also a hindrance to the Holy Spirit.

The landmark event had a lasting influence in the region. My church in Ashland, Kentucky, was possibly a part of the last vestige of the Cane Ridge phenomenon. I grew up hearing pastors and visiting evangelists who were mostly uneducated—that is, none that I know of had a college or university degree. But they knew their Bibles.

Agree or disagree, Spurgeon has been quoted as saying, "We cannot teach a person *how* to preach, but we can teach him *what* to preach." That said, the preacher can make mistakes. Huge mistakes. But what we have in Scripture is infallible, faithful, and absolutely true. God saw to that.

To put it another way, the Word of God in *print* and the Word of God in *person* have this in common: the divine and human factor. Jesus was God *as though* He were not man; He was man *as though* He were not God. "In the beginning was the Word, and the Word was with God, and the Word was God. . . . And the Word became flesh" (John 1:1, 14). Likewise, the Scriptures are from God *as though* apart from those who wrote it, and yet those who wrote it showed their personalities *as though* they were on their own and given full liberty to express what they felt and believed. Therefore, the Word of God incarnate and the Word of God in print have this in common. As Jesus was without sin and His words were without error, so too the Scriptures are doctrinally and theologically inerrant.

PERSONAL REFLECTION

What is your relationship like with your Bible? Did you grow up memorizing verses? Do you find it challenging to love the Word, or are you excited about reading the Scriptures?

_____

_____

_____

How do you handle passages in the Bible that you don't under-stand? If you could receive clarity from the Holy Spirit on one portion of Scripture, what would it be? Where do you go for strong expository teaching on God's Word?

_____

_____

_____

Have you ever felt confronted by God Himself through preaching of the Word? What was God showing you about Himself and His Word through the human personality of the teacher?

_____

_____

_____

THE INNER TESTIMONY OF THE SPIRIT

All Scripture is God-breathed [given by divine inspiration] and is
profitable for instruction, for conviction [of sin], for correction [of
error and restoration to obedience], for training in righteousness
[learning to live in conformity to God's will, both publicly and
privately—behaving honorably with personal integrity and moral
courage]; so that the man of God may be complete and proficient,
outfitted and thoroughly equipped for every good work.
—2 TIMOTHY 3:16–17, AMP

ONE OF THE greatest adjustments I have had to make—
and am still having to make—is to *assume nothing*
when I preach and when I write. I must keep in mind
that many of my hearers and readers—thank God for the excep-
tions—will need my help to grow in their understanding and
knowledge of Scripture.

It is a new generation, somewhat like the new pharaoh who
did not know Joseph (Exod. 1:8). There was a time when all
Egypt rejoiced in Joseph and his family, but that era did not last.
There came a new pharaoh who owed Joseph nothing, a new
generation who did not appreciate Joseph—indeed, a generation
who felt threatened by Joseph's legacy.

It is much like that today. So many people in the church do

not know their Bibles because they do not often read their Bibles. Not only that, church leaders themselves often do not know their Bibles; neither do they urgently encourage Bible reading. Worst of all, an ever-increasing number of people in the pulpit and pew have not been persuaded by the inner testimony of the Holy Spirit that the Bible is the Word of God.

This is how we know that the Bible is the Word of God: by the inner testimony of the Holy Spirit. There are those who have tried to lean on the so-called "external" proofs of Scripture—archaeology, testimonies of people who say what the Bible has meant to them, and so on. These external proofs will not totally persuade. Only the Holy Spirit totally persuades. And because there has been a diminishing of the knowledge of the Holy Spirit in our day, it is not surprising that many people are "tossed to and fro" by "every wind of doctrine" (Eph. 4:14).

I would say of the apostle Paul that his *letters* are infallible. He himself wasn't. He was only a man. Luke tells of when Paul lost his temper (see Acts 23:3), something Jesus never did. Paul was capable of making mistakes. But when he wrote his epistles, God overruled, and we can embrace Paul's words wholeheartedly. So too with Matthew, Mark, Luke, and John, as well as the Old Testament and all the rest of the New Testament writers. You may safely read all of Scripture, knowing that the same faithful God who sent His Son into the world to die on a cross made sure His Son's words were recorded without error and the apostles chosen to write what we call the New Testament gave us infallible teaching.

God would not send His Son to us and then allow what He came to do to be forgotten. That is why we have the Bible. God gave us our Bibles. Are you thankful for the Bible? Have you thought where we would be today without Bibles? If then God gave us Bibles, does He not want us to know what is in them?

The degree to which we believe the Bible is infallible, reliable, and faithful often determines how much we care to read it. Mind you, the church being in a deep sleep has resulted even in many advanced Christians being dormant in their Bible reading. As I said, I can recall a day—in my lifetime—when *laypeople* knew the Bible so well you could begin quoting a verse and many would finish it! In a previous generation not only did people read their Bibles, but they also memorized large portions of them. Such a practice has virtually perished from the earth today.

Some say, "What I need is to be slain in the Spirit." I say: if you are empty-headed when you fall, you will be empty-headed when you get up. There will be nothing in your head of which the Holy Spirit can remind you!

We need the Bible. However, I am also saying we need *more* than the Bible. We need the Holy Spirit. To quote Jack Taylor, there are those whose understanding of the Trinity is "God the Father, God the Son, and God the Holy Bible."[1] This candid observation is often accurate because of the presupposition that the Spirit and Word are inseparable. If the Holy Spirit does not intervene and *apply* what I teach and write, my efforts are in vain. God must step in, or no one is gripped, no one is converted.

In a word, Scripture needs to be *applied*. This comes about by anointed preaching. But anointed preaching is never possible without the power of the Holy Spirit.

Personal Reflection

How could you show your gratitude to God for the gift of His Word today? Whom do you know that has a high value for his or her Bible? In what ways does he or she practically prioritize Scripture?

_____

_____

_____

How would you arrange your day if Jesus appeared in the flesh in your living room? Do you believe that the Bible is infallible, reliable, and faithful? How could you arrange your day to reflect the reality of the value of God's Word in print?

_____

_____

_____

LOVE IS SPELLED T-I-M-E

I rise before dawn and cry for help;
I wait for Your words.
My eyes anticipate the night watches,
So that I may meditate on Your word.
—PSALM 119:147–148, NASB

I HAD A HEAD start in the matter of Christian living. My earliest memory of my father is seeing him on his knees for thirty minutes every morning before he went to work. He often read his Bible on his knees. He knew his Bible better than many preachers today and certainly prayed more than many preachers do today. It was the way he was brought up. He had a pastor who encouraged members of the church to spend thirty minutes a day in quiet time. He passed that heritage on to me and brought me up the same way. I am determined to pass this on as long as I have breath.

Martin Luther (1483–1546) endeavored to pray three hours every day. John Wesley (1703–1791) would not think of going into his daily work before he prayed two hours each day, usually rising at four o'clock in the morning.[1] According to a recent poll, participated in by thousands of church leaders on both sides of the Atlantic, the average church leader today—minister, evangelist, pastor, bishop, vicar, rector—spends *four minutes a day* in personal quiet time. And you wonder why the church is asleep.

How much do you pray? How much do you read your Bible? How well do you know your Bible?

Would you like to be on good terms with the Holy Spirit? Then get to know what He wrote! He wrote the Bible. He is not ashamed of what He wrote. The Bible is the Holy Spirit's greatest product. You will have the Holy Spirit's anointing to the degree that you honor what the Holy Spirit *wrote*.

"My people are destroyed for lack of knowledge," said the prophet (Hos. 4:6). God wants all of us to be well acquainted with especially two things about Him: His Word and His ways. His Word refers to the Bible—the Old and New Testaments. His ways refer to His characteristics. "They have not known my *ways*," God lamented of His ancient people (Heb. 3:10, emphasis added). Moses, being assured that his ways pleased the Lord and that he could ask for anything, requested, "Show me now your ways" (Exod. 33:13).

God has *ways*. The Holy Spirit has *ways*. You may not like His ways. Moreover, He will not adjust to you; you must adjust to Him. How does one get to know God's ways? How do you get to know anybody's way? Answer: by spending time with him or her.

Children spell love T-I-M-E. That is what they want more than anything—time with their parents, time with those they look up to. We show how much we esteem a person by how much time we give to him or her.

My wife knows my *ways*. She knows how I think. She knows how I will react to a book, a sermon, a political speech, or new people I meet. I have a handful of friends who truly know my ways. They have spent considerable time with me. Do not underestimate how well you get to know God's ways merely by spending time with Him.

I would urge you to spend thirty minutes a day alone with God. You can count the Bible reading as part of that, but remember that time spent with God is never wasted. The following sentence is attributed to Martin Luther, although I cannot find it in his writings: "I have so much to do that if I didn't spend at least three hours a day in prayer, I would never get it all done."[2] Whether he said these words or not, we know Luther was a man of prayer. The idea being expressed is that the busier he got, the more essential prayer became. Most of us would excuse ourselves from praying more if we had a busy day.

The principle is this: give God His 10 percent and live on the 90 percent you keep for yourself. My dad used to say, "I sometimes think the 90 percent even goes further than the 100 percent!" Likewise, the more time you give to God, the more you get done! I am assuming you will use common sense when I suggest these things; don't try to pray around the clock! I promise you, give God thirty minutes a day—one hour or more if you are in full-time ministry—and you will get more done than you would have had you neglected quiet time with the Lord. Even Jesus needed this. "And rising very early in the morning, while it was still dark, he departed and went out to a desolate place, and there he prayed" (Mark 1:35).

The time of day is not as important as choosing a time when you can be most alert and effective. If you are not a morning person, pray in the evenings. Time alone with the Lord will bring you closer to Him and enable you to get to know His ways.

Personal Reflection

Do you set aside a time daily to pray? If not, what seems to be your greatest hurdle to setting aside intentional time to spend with the Lord?

_____

_____

_____

How could you carve out consistent time to read the Word and pray? Once you begin this practice, make a note of the changes you observe in your emotional, mental, and spiritual life.

_____

_____

_____

ADJUSTING TO THE DOVE

For as many as are led by the Spirit of God,
these are sons of God.
—ROMANS 8:14, NKJV

M Y MOST CHERISHED insight at Westminster Chapel was to discover the sensitivity of the Holy Spirit. Arguably it is the most life-changing concept I have come across. I came to grasp this before I faced the challenge of totally forgiving those who hurt me and betrayed me. It was my awareness of the sensitivity of the Spirit that caused me to realize the importance of total forgiveness. The sensitivity of the Spirit and total forgiveness are reciprocal; they are truly inseparable. You grieve the Spirit when you don't forgive; when you totally forgive, the Holy Spirit will move into your heart with unfathomable peace and joy.

One essential feature of the Holy Spirit's ways is that He is—like it or not—a very, very sensitive person. The third member of the Trinity is a person, and one of His ways is that He gets His feelings hurt—easily. You may say, "He should not be like that." But that is the way He is. Get over it, or you will never get to know Him. He will not adjust to you; you must adjust to Him.

Years ago a British couple was sent by their denomination to be missionaries in Israel. After a few weeks in their new home near Jerusalem, they noticed that a dove had come to live in the eaves of their house. They also noticed that whenever they would slam a door, the dove would fly away. Every time they got into an argument with each other, the dove would fly away. One day Sandy said to Bernice, "Have you noticed the dove?"

"Oh yes," she replied. "It is like a seal of God on our being in Israel."

Sandy noted how the dove would fly away every time they slammed a door shut or got into a heated argument. "I'm so afraid the dove will fly away and never come back," Bernice said.

Then Sandy looked at her and said, "Either the dove adjusts to us, or we adjust to the dove." They changed their lives—just to keep the dove around.

Doves are gentle, loving, and afraid of people. You cannot get physically close to a dove; it will fly away before you can touch it.

Like a dove, the Holy Spirit is easily grieved and quenched. Like it or not, *the easiest thing in the world to do is to grieve the Holy Spirit*. You may need time to absorb the previous sentence, but believe me, it is not an exaggeration.

The bottom line is this: the Holy Spirit is indeed a very sensitive person. When Paul said, "Do not *grieve* the Holy Spirit" (Eph. 4:30, emphasis added), he used a Greek word that means to get your feelings hurt.[1] The Holy Spirit gets His feelings hurt very, very easily.

The greatest challenge I have *ever* faced is to try to go a day or two without grieving the Spirit. You do it when you do not mean to; you do it when you try not to! You may say, "That's not fair." I understand because I have thought that a thousand times. But that is one of the *ways* of the Holy Spirit.

I have come to understand this aspect of the Holy Spirit by spending more and more time with Him. The more I get to know Him, the more I see how sinful I am—so frail, weak, pitiful, and unworthy. I have also discovered that you rarely know it at the time when you grieve the Spirit. You feel nothing when you make the unguarded comment to a friend or stranger, show your frustration with the old woman at the cash register in a supermarket who has all day and you are in a hurry, speak impatiently on the phone with a terse airline representative, honk your horn at the slow car in front of you, or say an unkind word about someone. "I told the truth," you may say. Granted, but you still grieved the Holy Spirit; the dove flies away for the moment.

The more time we spend with God, the more we see His holiness and our sin. It is not that the Holy Spirit ever deserts us when we stumble; no, He never leaves us (John 14:16). But we lose the *sense* of His presence: clear thinking, insight into a difficult verse in the Bible, knowing what grieves the Spirit.

God is gracious and forgiving. But He wants us to know His ways. Getting to know His ways means spending time with Him. There may be shortcuts, but I have not found them.

PERSONAL REFLECTION

Is there anyone that comes to mind as you read today's devotional that you have yet to totally forgive? Take some time right

now to ask the Holy Spirit to bring to mind anything about your
life that could be grievous to Him.

_____

_____

_____

Imagine the Holy Spirit as a live dove resting on your shoulder
as you journey throughout your day. How would you speak to
others? What would you watch on television? What would you
adjust, knowing that One so sensitive was resting upon you?

_____

_____

_____

A Greater Measure

The Spirit of the LORD will rest on him—the Spirit of
wisdom and of understanding, the Spirit of counsel and of
might, the Spirit of the knowledge and fear of the LORD.
—ISAIAH 11:2, NIV

WOULD YOU LIKE more of the Holy Spirit? I certainly would. Some people might object to the idea of "more" of the Holy Spirit. They take the view that either you have all there is of the Holy Spirit, or you don't. That is a superficial observation—and very misleading indeed. The thrust of all the New Testament letters is about increasing our faith, getting closer to God, and getting more of Him. Only Jesus had the Holy Spirit without limit (John 3:34). You and I have but a "measure" of the Spirit, which is why we have a measure of faith (Rom. 12:3).

The disciples asked of Jesus, "Increase our faith!" (Luke 17:5). As one man put it, "I believe; help my unbelief!" (Mark 9:24). You and I are often in this very position; we struggle but want God to increase our faith. This comes in proportion to getting a greater measure of the Holy Spirit.

The following teaching might seem directed to preachers or leaders, but *all* Christians—men and women, young and old—need it. If you are not a pastor or leader, this still applies to you, whatever your job, gift, or calling may be. It might also help you gain an appreciation for the responsibility your pastor and church leaders carry and cause you to pray harder for them. All readers will benefit from what follows.

Do not take what I say in these lines as being from an expert. I said at the beginning that I did not see the Holy Spirit work in my ministry as I hoped—and still pray for. What follows are suggestions. They have led me to the little bit of anointing I have. God has not finished with me yet. But here is what I put to you.

If you want more of the Holy Spirit, first, ask for it. Paul requested that the Ephesians pray for him to be given "words" when he spoke (6:19). Jesus said that we should ask and the Father will give the Holy Spirit to us. (See Luke 11:9–13 and James 4:2.)

Readers of my book *Holy Fire* might recall my life-changing experience of the Holy Spirit when driving from Palmer, Tennessee, to Nashville on October 31, 1955. What happened came as a result of my *asking* for more of God. To my amazement—I have never gotten over it—I suddenly witnessed Jesus interceding for me at the right hand of God the Father. After being in the Spirit for an hour, I literally heard these words of Jesus to the Father: "He wants it." The Father replied, "He can have it." Immediately a warm surge of the Spirit entered my heart. A peace I did not know was possible in this life was given to me. It changed my life and also my theology. I have never been the same since.

Second, if you want a greater measure of the Spirit, spend

time pleading with God and waiting for Him to act. You might ask, "But how can I know God's ways merely by spending time with Him?" The answer is, *because you do*! Spending time alone with God honors Him and affirms His Word and His promise. When you do this, part of the reward is beginning to know His ways. You reap this benefit merely by consciously spending time with Him, boring though it might seem at the time.

It is wonderful to know God's ways. This means you are coming to know God in a way that ancient Israel didn't! God lamented, "They have not known my ways" (Heb. 3:10). But God will not say this of *you* when you take time to spend time with Him.

The power comes not from how much I know, how much I read commentaries and books, or how much time I spend in fellowship with godly friends. It comes from seeking God's face in the equivalent of a "tent of meeting." (See Exodus 33:7, 9, 11.)

Intimacy with God comes by making an effort and spending as much time with Him as you can. Never forget that He is a jealous God (Exod. 20:5). If you do not like this aspect of God's nature, I'm sorry, but that is simply the way He is. God wants you to love Him for being *just like He is*.

I can make this promise to you: get to know Him by spending time with Him, and you will find yourself overwhelmed with amazement that we have a God like Him.

Personal Reflection

Take some time right now to ask the Lord for a greater measure of His Spirit. What do you feel or sense from Him when you ask that? Don't be impatient for an answer; wait on Him.

_____

_____

_____

How has the presence of the Holy Spirit manifested in your life? Have you experienced His presence in your physical body or maybe in waves of peace or an inner knowing? Spend some time thanking the Lord for whatever way His Spirit has revealed Himself to you.

_____

_____

_____

NO SHORTCUTS

> Now, the "Lord" I'm referring to is the Holy Spirit, and wherever he is Lord, there is freedom. We can all draw close to him with the veil removed from our faces. And with no veil we all become like mirrors who brightly reflect the glory of the Lord Jesus. We are being transfigured into his very image as we move from one brighter level of glory to another. And this glorious transfiguration comes from the Lord, who is the Spirit.
> —2 CORINTHIANS 3:17–18, TPT

IF YOU AND I truly want to get on good terms with the Holy Spirit, we will not be able to take shortcuts. It takes time, but the effort is worth it!

You will want to know your Bible backward and forward. You almost certainly should begin with a Bible reading plan. Any will do, but it should be one that takes you through the Bible in a year. My Robert Murray M'Cheyne (1813–1843) Bible reading plan takes me through the Psalms and the New Testament twice a year.

Those in the ministry should read the Bible not merely with a view of getting a sermon or even a "rhema word." Read it for its own sake. Get to know it. Know the patriarchs—Abraham, Isaac, Jacob, and Joseph. Know the history of Israel. Get to understand God's dealings with Moses.

Learn the place of the Law in God's scheme of redemption. Know the Psalms and the Prophets. Understand the teachings of Jesus. Be acquainted with the miracles and how the Holy Spirit came down on the day of Pentecost. See and grasp the history of the early church in the Book of Acts. Fall in love with the writings of Paul and all the apostles. You are reading God's own Word.

There is no knowledge under the sun that is equal to a vast knowledge of Holy Scripture. I would not trade my knowledge of the Bible for any amount of money or with the most learned physicist, philosopher, or physician in this world. What I have you can have. Anybody can have this. It is obtained by simply reading the Bible so much that you get to know it—all over.

I will make a second promise to you: *you will never be sorry you spent time with God's Word.* Whether you are a minister or a cab driver, a children's pastor or a restaurant server, a worship leader or an accountant—I could go on and on—get to know your Bible better than any other book. The reward is incalculable. Being on good terms with the Holy Spirit is greater than being connected to celebrities, royalty, or the president. Never forget what the great evangelist Dwight L. Moody (1837–1899) said: "The Bible was not given to increase our knowledge, but to change our lives."[1]

One might think this goes without saying, but if you want more of the Holy Spirit, you must also live a holy life. None of us are naturally prone to *want* holiness. *Holiness* and *sanctification* (the process by which we become holier) may be used interchangeably. We are all congenitally allergic to holiness! If the robust desire for holiness were automatic with faith in Christ, we would not need the epistles of the New Testament.

The reason we have the epistles is that seeking after holiness—sanctification—must be *taught*.

The New Testament doctrine of sanctification is the doctrine of gratitude. It is our way of saying, "Thank You, Lord, for saving my soul." Gratitude is sometimes spontaneous, but often it is not. Jesus healed ten lepers, but *only one* came back to say thank you. Jesus' immediate observation: "Where are the nine?" (Luke 17:17). This tells me three things: (1) God loves gratitude; He is honored when we take time to thank Him. (2) God hates ingratitude; He puts it alongside the most heinous sins (Rom. 1:21–32; 2 Tim. 3:2). (3) And gratitude must be taught.

We need to be taught and reminded to be grateful, just as Paul reminded his followers: "Give thanks in all circumstances" (1 Thess. 5:18). Likewise, holiness must be taught: "For this is the will of God, your sanctification" (1 Thess. 4:3).

In a word, if you want to be on good terms with the Spirit of God, remember that He is the *Holy* Spirit and that He wrote the Old and New Testaments. The epistles of the New Testament could be summed up as showing the necessity of holiness and how to live the holy life.

PERSONAL REFLECTION

Have you ever completed a Bible reading plan? What did you enjoy about it, and what was challenging about sticking to a schedule? How could you increase your intentional study of Scripture?

_____

_____

_____

What was the last thing you thanked God for? Spend some time today and list out as many things as you can think of in your life for which to give Him thanks. Ask the Holy Spirit if there is any area of your life where He wants to give you an upgrade in holiness.

_____

_____

_____

A GREATER ANOINTING

If you love me, keep my commands. And I will ask the
Father, and he will give you another advocate to help you and
be with you forever—the Spirit of truth. The world cannot
accept him, because it neither sees him nor knows him. But
you know him, for he lives with you and will be in you.
—JOHN 14:15–17, NIV

YEARS AGO, A British lawyer came into my vestry at
Westminster Chapel to say, "I believe I am called to
preach." I suggested that he test this call by joining us
in witnessing to lost people in the streets of Westminster on
Saturday morning. He immediately replied, "I am no good at
witnessing to one person, but I am good at speaking to thousands." I replied to him as gently as I could, "If you are not
willing to witness to one person, you are not called to witness
from a pulpit to thousands." He never came back again.

Within a few weeks of becoming the minister of
Westminster Chapel, I asked the congregation, "How many
of you out there have *never* led a soul to Jesus Christ?" I was
speaking to our regular church members when I asked this.
But I could equally address those in the ministry with the
same question! A minister who cannot witness to a person

on a one-to-one basis is—in my honest opinion—not fit to be preaching the Gospel from the pulpit.

We are all called to do this. If we see the lost start coming to Christ by the millions, I believe it will happen because the sleeping giant called the body of Christ wakes up, gets fired up, and starts talking about Jesus Christ to their neighbors, friends, and everyone they meet.

There is nothing like witnessing for Jesus Christ to bring about intimacy with God—that is, if intimacy with the Holy Spirit is what you want.

It is my view that the church today is asleep. That was Jesus' assessment of the church in the very last days—asleep. Having described the last days in Matthew 24, Jesus said in Matthew 25:1, "Then"—at that time, during the very last days—"the kingdom of heaven will be like ten virgins." Five were wise, and five were foolish, but they *all* slumbered and slept (v. 5). Yes, that is the best way I know to describe the church today—asleep. In the natural world you don't know you were asleep until you wake up. The same truth applies in the spiritual world. We—the body of Christ, the church— don't know we are asleep spiritually. We will not realize we have been sleeping until we wake up.

When the midnight cry described in Matthew 25 occurs, we will awaken and unashamedly witness for Jesus Christ to everyone—friends, neighbors, and strangers. Unfortunately, for now, a spirit of fear virtually paralyzes the church and keeps us in spiritual slumber.

My point is this: if it is power you want, try talking to people about Jesus wherever you go.

In addition to being a bold witness, if you want to increase your relationship with the Holy Spirit, make sure that you are seeking honor and praise from God, not people. John 5:44 has been my life verse for almost sixty-five years: "How can you believe, who receive honor from one another, and do not seek the honor that comes from the only God?" (NKJV). I am not sure why it has remained with me lifelong, but I know it first gripped me back in 1956 because two of my mentors often quoted it. When I say "life verse," I don't mean to suggest for one minute that I have lived up to this verse. I have failed many times, but I have sought to live by it.

John 5:44 shows that we should live and speak before an audience of one—namely, God alone. Malachi 3:16 says that God eavesdrops on our conversations. If we start speaking to one another with the awareness that God Himself is listening, it might drastically change the tenor of our conversations.

John 5:44 reveals the reason the Jews missed their Messiah: they were addicted to the approval of fellow Jews. They did not want to lose a friend by admitting that Jesus of Nazareth was the Messiah of God. Had they been motivated by the honor that comes from the only God—as they should have been— they would have been motivated not by fear of one another but by the fear of God. This goes to show that you and I could miss what God is doing today if we are more worried about what people think than what God thinks. Be motivated by the honor and praise that comes from God alone!

Finally, if we want more of the Holy Spirit, we also must esteem the *fruit* of the Spirit as much as the *gifts* of the Spirit and vice versa. It has been my observation that Spirit people tend to emphasize the gifts of the Spirit. Some feel the gifts are decidedly more important; we should talk about the gifts—often speaking in tongues. I'm sorry, but I run into a lot of Charismatic Christians that want to talk only about speaking in tongues and praying in tongues. They sometimes give the impression that they are a cut above those who don't speak in tongues. Some of them also tend to take the fruit of the Spirit for granted.

Word people seem to emphasize the fruit of the Spirit. They tend to go quiet when it comes to the gifts. It seems to make some of them nervous!

For many Word people, speaking in tongues is about the most offensive thing on the planet! With some denominations, for example, you can commit adultery, be divorced several times, and be a Freemason, and you will be forgiven. But if the word leaks out that you speak in tongues, you are immediately kept at a distance, held in suspicion, and kept at bay indefinitely! I wish it were not true. And yet we must be willing to accept the stigma that comes with being unashamed of the gift of speaking or praying in tongues. I don't mean to be unfair, but speaking personally, it is part of the price to pay if we want a greater anointing of the Spirit. Being kept at bay—or even rejected—is worth the price for a greater anointing. Would you not want a greater anointing than anything in the world?

PERSONAL REFLECTION

How does the idea of witnessing for Jesus Christ make you feel? What do you think stands in your way of sharing with others about the Gospel? If you're experiencing fear of man, take some time to repent and make the commitment to live for an audience of one. Ask the Lord if there is anyone whom He would have you share something with today.

_____

_____

_____

Take some time to review the fruit of the Spirit as well as the gifts of the Spirit. Do you think that you have focused on either one of those at the cost of the other?

_____

_____

_____

THE FRUIT OF THE SPIRIT—LOVE

> But the fruit of the Spirit is love, joy, peace, patience,
> kindness, goodness, faithfulness, gentleness, self-
> control; against such things there is no law.
> —GALATIANS 5:22–23, NASB

THE FRUIT—NOT *FRUITS*—OF the Spirit springs from obedience. The fruit of the Spirit is a requirement of all believers. Whereas the gifts of the Spirit, which we will explore on days 13–16, are sovereignly bestowed (1 Cor. 12:11, 18) and are irrevocable (Rom. 11:29), the fruit of the Spirit is what you and I are obliged to pursue.

The fruit of the Holy Spirit is the effect, or result, of living the Christian life in obedience. It is what *flows* in those who resist the "works of the flesh," namely, "sexual immorality, impurity, sensuality, idolatry, sorcery, enmity, strife, jealousy, fits of anger, rivalries, dissensions, divisions, envy, drunkenness, orgies" (Gal. 5:19–21). Those who give in to the works of the flesh forfeit their inheritance in the kingdom of God (v. 21).

To put it another way, the genuinely saved person has no choice; the fruit of the Spirit is a command.

Love is listed first. Why? Possibly because showing *agape* love will likely incorporate all the other qualities on Paul's list.

Three Greek words are translated as love: (1) *agape* is unselfish, self-giving love; (2) *eros* is physical love; and (3) *philia* is brotherly love. Galatians 5:22 uses *agape* love. If you truly experience this love, you will have joy, peace, patience, kindness, goodness, faithfulness, gentleness, and self-control. We find the proof in 1 Corinthians 13, where Paul unpacks the meaning of *agape* love. Once you grasp 1 Corinthians 13, you will discover that everything Paul calls the "fruit of the Spirit" is beautifully woven into 1 Corinthians 13.

I must also state the two ways the fruit of the Spirit manifests:

1. Spontaneously: Strange as it may seem, sometimes love just erupts! Like a geyser that shoots out water without provocation or cause, love sometimes flows with no effort on our part. It comes easily. The Holy Spirit does this.

2. By an act of the will: On the other hand, the same person who experienced this love spontaneously yesterday struggles today. What do you do? You intentionally force yourself to keep no record of wrongs; you refuse to point the finger. You work at it. But *because* you have the Holy Spirit, *you can do it*. Yesterday it was easy. Today it is not easy.

   Why? I believe that sometimes the Holy Spirit is simply waiting for *us* to make an effort. Either way, the result is to demonstrate to others that you truly show the fruit of the Spirit.

The kind of love listed in the fruit of the Spirit is a self-sacri-ficing, unselfish love. It is the love that lies behind God sending His Son into the world (John 3:16). It is perhaps best summed up in 1 Corinthians 13:5: love "keeps no record of wrongs" (NIV). Why do we keep records? To prove we have paid our bills. Why keep a record of wrongs? To bring up the past, to point the finger, to make a person feel guilty. When you experience *agape* love, you do not bring up one's guilty past. Just as God forgives, you forgive. It is the first fruit Paul mentions. The other qualities follow love, according to Paul.

There are also occasions when the fruit-of-the-Spirit love is manifested apart from the act of forgiveness. There are times when the dove comes down on us spontaneously without our consciously having to forgive by an act of the will. God may choose to show up when we are not even praying! He is both sovereign and gracious. The love that flows from the Spirit can even be experienced by refusing to give in to *any* temptation of the flesh—including sexual temptation, greed, or jealousy. The same fruit of the Spirit will often manifest through our digni-fying a trial. In other words, instead of complaining and grum-bling when a trial suddenly comes, we submit to it—as it "falleth from above," as the hymn "Like a River Glorious" puts it.

The same can be said for other fruit of the Spirit. Whereas consciously forgiving others will result in love, joy, and peace, we may nonetheless discover such fruit of the Spirit because our lives are being directed by a sovereign, gracious God.

PERSONAL REFLECTION

Have you experienced spontaneous love for someone, where love simply erupts in your heart without explanation? Take some time to remember this moment. Ask the Lord what He was teaching you about His nature and His kingdom through this experience.

_____

_____

_____

Have you experienced the deliberate choice to love someone when it's not easy to do so? Take some time to remember the moment you chose to love. Ask the Lord what He was teaching you about the fruit of the Spirit and His intentional love.

_____

_____

_____

JOY, PEACE, PATIENCE, KINDNESS

But the fruit produced by the Holy Spirit within you is
divine love in all its varied expressions: joy that overflows,
peace that subdues, patience that endures, kindness in
action, a life full of virtue, faith that prevails, gentleness
of heart, and strength of spirit. Never set the law above
these qualities, for they are meant to be limitless.
—GALATIANS 5:22–23, TPT

JOY IS AN internal feeling of great pleasure. The difference
between joy and happiness is that joy is internal; happiness
comes from external things that make us feel good—a kind
letter, a raise in pay, a compliment. Joy, however, is internal. This
pleasure flows from voluntarily refusing to point the finger at
someone else. It is an act of the will.

When I refuse to point the finger—difficult though it may
sometimes be—the result is sooner or later the same: joy.
Internal pleasure. I feel good that I resisted pointing the finger.
It is as though the Spirit rewards me for keeping no record of
wrongs. But as I said before, one may experience joy by refusing
to complain or not giving in to any temptations of the flesh.

Like love, joy can come either by an act of the will (as I've
just described) or spontaneously. Years ago, I experienced spontaneous joy while driving my car from Palmer, Tennessee, to

Nashville. It is quite impossible to describe. It was truly "joy unspeakable and full of glory" (1 Pet. 1:8, KJV). It lasted a good while, but one day—suddenly—it ended. After that I had to get my joy from voluntarily, actively, and intentionally overlooking faults in others that bother me. Or refusing to grumble. Or not speaking evil of another person—even if what I might have said was true! One can state what may well be true about another, but we will grieve the Spirit if our motive is to make another look bad.

Now you understand what I meant when I said that the fruit of the Spirit is sometimes spontaneous and sometimes by an act of the will. However, as I said, it is because you *have* the Holy Spirit that you can produce the same fruit by an act of your will.

Peace is equally difficult to describe. It is not merely the absence of anxiety; it is the undeniable presence of a calm feeling deep inside. Calm is perhaps the best word to describe it. It is a feeling of self-control—a fruit that Paul includes at the end of the list. You cannot turn on instant peace by an act of the will, but you can do what leads to it by intentionally overlooking another's faults, refusing to point the finger, and telling God alone—not others—what you feel (Ps. 142:2).

Patience is the steadfastness to endure pain, delay, or trouble without getting angry or upset. Again, sometimes this is given with spontaneous ease; other times you force yourself not to complain. This is why James said we should *count* it—impute to the trial—pure joy when we fall into various kinds of trouble (Jas. 1:2). James added, "And let steadfastness have its full effect, that you may be perfect and complete, lacking in nothing" (v. 4).

Peter has his own list of qualities, similar to Paul's but not in the same order.

> For this very reason, make every effort to supplement your faith with virtue, and virtue with knowledge, and knowledge with self-control, and self-control with steadfastness, and steadfastness with godliness, and godliness with brotherly affection, and brotherly affection with love. For if these qualities are yours and are increasing, they keep you from being ineffective or unfruitful in the knowledge of our Lord Jesus Christ.
>
> —2 Peter 1:5–8

This passage shows that the order of the listed virtues is not of supreme importance; it shows how the minds of two godly men work differently. Also, whereas Paul lists some of these qualities as "fruit" of the Spirit, Peter puts the onus on us as if we are responsible for such a pursuit. The point is, the fruit of the Spirit listed by Paul and the qualities listed by Peter are what you and I are commanded to display.

There is a difference between the *fruit* of the Spirit and the *gifts* of the Spirit. You and I are *required* to manifest love, patience, and brotherly affection; we are not required to have the gift of miracles or discerning of spirits, as we will see in day 13.

The writer of Hebrews wrote to discouraged Jewish believers, "You have need of endurance" (10:36). Don't we all? Sometimes such a virtue flows passively without effort; other times, as I have been saying, we must make an effort to do these things because we do have the Holy Spirit.

Paul said, "Love is patient and kind" (1 Cor. 13:4). Kindness means being considerate, friendly, or nice. I have learned that kindness goes very far in winning people over to your position. In the days I met with Yasser Arafat (1929–2004) and some

Palestinians, I learned one thing for sure: our *doctrine* will not win them; showing that we care will win them. That's it. When they feel this from us, they are far more apt to listen to what we have to say.

This is why James makes a huge point, namely, that the "poor man" (2:6) will not be impressed by our sound teaching but by our showing good works. James asked, "Can that faith save [the poor man]?" (v. 14). Answer: no, but our kindness is more likely to win him over.

Kindness, then, is a fruit of the Holy Spirit—even if you have to remind yourself to be kind!

PERSONAL REFLECTION

Consider the moments or seasons in your life when you have experienced the most joy. How much of your joy was the result of spontaneous feeling, and how much was the result of deliberate decisions on your part? What choices have you made that have filled you with the most joy?

_____

_____

_____

Where do you feel the Holy Spirit stretching you to grow in fruitfulness? Do peace, patience, and kindness come easily to you, or do they come with more of an effort on your part? Ask the Holy Spirit to fill you today with an increased measure of His empowering grace!

_____

_____

_____

GOODNESS, FAITHFULNESS, GENTLENESS, SELF-CONTROL

But the fruit of the Spirit [the result of His presence within us] is love [unselfish concern for others], joy, [inner] peace, patience [not the ability to wait, but how we act while waiting], kindness, goodness, faithfulness, gentleness, self-control. Against such things there is no law.
—GALATIANS 5:22–23, AMP

GOODNESS MEANS, SIMPLY, being good, being decent, showing unselfishness. It's when we make an effort to do something helpful. We often use the expression "That is good of you to do." It is the opposite of being bad, wicked, or immoral.

Luke says of Barnabas that he was "a good man" (Acts 11:24). For a human being to be called "a good man" in Holy Writ, you may safely mark it down that Barnabas was unusual. Those who knew Barnabas held him with such respect that when all were keenly suspicious of Saul of Tarsus—even after Saul's conversion—Barnabas was able to cause others to accept him (9:27). The disciples were first called Christians in Antioch when Barnabas was around (11:26).

When I first went to Trevecca Nazarene University in

Nashville in 1953, I remember going to a store to buy something. I realized I forgot to bring money. The manager of the store said, "Did you say you were from Trevecca?" I responded in the affirmative. "Then you have good credit here. We all know those people are good." What a reputation!

Faithfulness means being trustworthy, being loyal, having integrity. A husband who is faithful is one who avoids sexual activity with another woman. Yes, a faithful man, who can find? Take loyalty, for example. I have come to the conclusion that there is no way one can know in advance whether a person will be loyal. I know of no test one can take, no question put in an interview, that will help you determine whether a person will be faithful. A leader needs an assistant who will be loyal; a wife needs a husband who will be faithful; a wealthy person needs someone around him or her who not only has wisdom but also will be trustworthy.

In any case, the fruit of the Spirit results in a person having the rare quality of integrity. Think about this for a moment. A person who follows the Holy Spirit will not cheat, lie, or betray. Yet, sadly, many church leaders today are discovered to be lacking in financial integrity or sexual faithfulness. Whatever else this indicates, it shows that such a person lacks the fruit of the Holy Spirit. If all Christians consistently obeyed the Lord by showing the fruit of the Spirit, there would be no unfaithfulness, sexual immorality, disloyalty, or mistrust in the church!

Gentleness comes from a Greek word meaning mild and sometimes translated as "meekness."[1] The funny thing is, in the Greco-Roman world this was no quality to be admired!

Quite the opposite; the Greeks saw this as being cowardly and weak.

The Christian faith, however, has taken over this word to make it something to be not only admired but also sought after. Jesus said, "Blessed are the meek" (Matt. 5:5). Meekness means that you won't be defensive if someone speaks against you. You will take criticism lying down. You will turn the other cheek.

Gentleness, then, means being mild-mannered or tender. Love is "not easily provoked" (1 Cor. 13:5, KJV), "not irritable" (ESV). Jesus said of Himself, "I am gentle and lowly in heart" (Matt. 11:29). Moses was "very meek, more than all people who were on the face of the earth" (Num. 12:3).

Meekness is not a quality the ancient Greeks admired. In today's world it is certainly not the way you win elections if in politics! However, it is a fruit of the Holy Spirit, and if you and I follow the Spirit with all our hearts, we will display this fruit of gentleness.

Self-control comes from the Greek word *egkrateia*. It denotes "the virtue of one who masters his desires and passions, especially his sensual appetites."[2] It was reckoned to be a cardinal virtue by Socrates (c. 470–399 BC). For Philo (c. 20 BC–AD 50) it meant superiority to every desire. It was expressed in restraint relating to food, sex, and use of the tongue. Paul used it regarding an athlete: "Every athlete exercises self-control in all things" (1 Cor. 9:25).

The fact that it is a fruit of the Holy Spirit is challenging for most of us. We all need self-control—whether in regard to eating, exercising, watching television, or taking time off when we are working too hard. Because we have the Holy

Spirit, says Paul, we *can* control how much we eat and whether we exercise, resist temptation, or give in to pleasure. It is surprising that we don't see this word more often. It is not in the four Gospels. It is also remarkable that Paul lists this fruit at the bottom of his list! He might have put it first!

The King James Version wrongly translates the Greek as "temperance," which brings to mind the old movement against legalizing alcohol in the United States. Don't let that mislead you into thinking this is about avoiding alcohol. The fruit of the Spirit will enable us to resist overdoing *anything*—whatever habit or temptation—that militates against godliness.

We are not responsible for having the gifts of the Spirit, but—like it or not—we are responsible for having the fruit of the Spirit.

PERSONAL REFLECTION

Think back to a few people in your life about whom you would say, "That was a good man or woman." What qualities did they possess that would cause you to say that about them? How did their goodness impact your life?

_____

_____

_____

Proverbs points out that faithfulness is a rare quality in a person. (See Proverbs 20:6.) Have you experienced the loyalty of a friend or family member? How did that make you feel? Have you showed up in a moment of crisis with faithfulness toward another?

_____

_____

_____

What do you think is the difference between meekness and weakness? Where does self-control manifest in your life?

_____

_____

_____

COVET THE GIFTS OF THE SPIRIT

Now concerning spiritual gifts, brethren, I do not want you to be ignorant: You know that you were Gentiles, carried away to these dumb idols, however you were led. Therefore I make known to you that no one speaking by the Spirit of God calls Jesus accursed, and no one can say that Jesus is Lord except by the Holy Spirit. There are diversities of gifts, but the same Spirit. There are differences of ministries, but the same Lord. And there are diversities of activities, but it is the same God who works all in all. But the manifestation of the Spirit is given to each one for the profit of all: for to one is given the word of wisdom through the Spirit, to another the word of knowledge through the same Spirit, to another faith by the same Spirit, to another gifts of healings by the same Spirit, to another the working of miracles, to another prophecy, to another discerning of spirits, to another different kinds of tongues, to another the interpretation of tongues. But one and the same Spirit works all these things, distributing to each one individually as He wills.
—1 Corinthians 12:1–11, nkjv

WHEREAS ALL BELIEVERS are commanded to manifest the *fruit* of the Spirit, the *gifts* of the Spirit are sovereignly bestowed on various people in the body of Christ by God. However, if you believe you are exempt from earnestly desiring the gifts of the Spirit, I answer: if you do not want them, I question whether you have the Holy Spirit at all. I firmly believe that if you have the Holy Spirit, you are going to welcome the pursuit of the *fruit* of the Spirit. Likewise, if you have the same Holy Spirit in you, you will take Paul's word seriously—to "covet" the *gifts* of the Spirit (1 Cor. 12:31, KJV).

The Greek word *zēloō* means "to burn with zeal" or "be zealous."[1] Paul uses this word in 1 Corinthians 12:31 to instruct us to be zealous in wanting the gifts of the Spirit. There is a scholarly debate whether *zēloō* is in the imperative mood, thus meaning a command, or in the present tense, thus acknowledging what these Corinthians already coveted. Either way, it shows what people of the Spirit want—or should want!

The fruit of the Spirit is a demonstration to the world that we are different from the world. The world knows nothing of *agape* love, inner joy, and peace—not to mention self-control. The gifts of the Spirit are bestowed not only for our *effectiveness* in the world but also for *edifying* the body of Christ. The gifts are for the "common good" of the church (1 Cor. 12:7).

In my book *Holy Fire* I refute the notion that the gifts of the Spirit ceased centuries ago (nobody knows when) by God's decree. If that were so, the fruit of the Spirit should also cease!

Thankfully neither ceased. If Jesus Christ is the same yesterday, today, and forever (Heb. 13:8), so too is the Holy Spirit the same yesterday, today, and forever. God is the same. He does not change (Mal. 3:6). The commands of Scripture do not change. We are responsible for them all.

For example, when a new Christian begins reading the Bible, he or she will read it thinking that God is still all-powerful and can and does do anything! How sad when someone says to this new convert, "Oh, by the way, you can't believe all of the Bible." Liberals say that!

Why is it that Word people emphasize the fruit of the Spirit but seem to be shy when speaking of the gifts? I answer again: because of tongues. That's it. Nothing more. If there were no mention of the gift of tongues in 1 Corinthians 12, there would never have been a cessationist teaching. Tongues is where the offense is. My colleague Charles Carrin says, "Tongues is the only spiritual gift deliberately designed to attack man's ego and pride."[2] There is no stigma when it comes to the other gifts: wisdom, knowledge, faith, miracles, prophecy. Who wouldn't welcome any of these? But because of *tongues*, which can be so embarrassing, one has to eliminate these greater gifts! And it is the greater gifts—the "higher gifts" (1 Cor. 12:31)—we are to earnestly desire.

Someone will no doubt say, "Since the gift of tongues is at the bottom of the list, that shows it is not important." Wrong. We just saw that self-control—a very important fruit indeed—is at the bottom of Paul's list of the fruit of the Spirit. I do agree that wisdom is a higher gift than speaking in tongues, but *all* the gifts listed are important and valuable.

I say to anyone who wants as much of the Holy Spirit as you can get: *be willing to start at the bottom—where the stigma is—if you really and truly want more of the Holy Spirit!* Do you want the gift of wisdom? Be willing to start at the bottom! Would you like the gift of healing? Be prepared to start at the bottom if you truly covet the gifts of the Holy Spirit as God's Word instructs you to.

Personal Reflection

What has your experience been like with the spiritual gifts? Have you known people who have operated in them? Have you seen them in operation in your own life? What has been the result?

_____

_____

_____

Do you agree that the gift of tongues can be embarrassing? Why do you think that is? Spend some time with God, praying about the spiritual gifts. Which gift do you long to see moving in your life? How would this gift change the world around you?

_____

_____

_____

Day 14

THE GIFTS OF WISDOM, KNOWLEDGE, AND FAITH

Consider it pure joy, my brothers and sisters, whenever you face trials of many kinds, because you know that the testing of your faith produces perseverance. Let perseverance finish its work so that you may be mature and complete, not lacking anything. If any of you lacks wisdom, you should ask God, who gives generously to all without finding fault, and it will be given to you. But when you ask, you must believe and not doubt, because the one who doubts is like a wave of the sea, blown and tossed by the wind. That person should not expect to receive anything from the Lord. Such a person is double-minded and unstable in all they do.
—JAMES 1:2–8, NIV

WISDOM IS FIRST on Paul's list, and it is called "the utterance of wisdom" (1 Cor. 12:8). The King James Version says "word of wisdom." It is possible for this to be a permanent bestowal on a person or something that is given once in an instance. In other words, some may have a permanent gift and always show wisdom in what they say. Others may have a one-off utterance of wisdom when it is needed. *Utterance* comes from *logos*, meaning "word."

It is interesting that wisdom is not a fruit of the Spirit! It is also interesting that the original seven deacons were to be men "full of the Spirit *and* of wisdom" (Acts 6:3, emphasis added), suggesting that a person can be full of the Spirit and still not have wisdom. This notion does not surprise me; I have seen people who were full of the Spirit but very unwise!

Wisdom, then, is a gift of the Spirit. However, quite apart from being a gift of the Holy Spirit, wisdom is on offer to all. We are to pray for wisdom, according to James 1:5. Furthermore, according to Proverbs 9:10, the way forward for wisdom is "the fear of the LORD." It has nothing to do with one's IQ or status.

The Greek word is *sophia*,[1] thought by the ancient Greeks to be out of reach for ordinary people. Only people such as Plato, Socrates, and Aristotle could have *sophia*. The early Greeks were cessationists before their time!

However, the New Testament offers wisdom to *anyone*. Wisdom is having the presence of the mind of the Spirit. It is knowing what to do next—the next step forward in what God has in mind for you. It is 20/20 foresight vision. We all have 20/20 hindsight vision ("If only I had done that!"), but if you have the mind of the Holy Spirit, you will get it right in advance.

Wisdom is the paramount and supreme gift. *Get it*, "though it cost all you have" (Prov. 4:7, NIV). It is the highest, greatest, and most important gift. The apostles had it in the early church and required it of the seven original deacons. Paul lists it first when mentioning the gifts of the Holy Spirit.

The gift of knowledge is called "utterance of knowledge" in the English Standard Version, "word of knowledge" in the King James Version, and "message of knowledge" in the New International Version.

There is a difference between wisdom and knowledge. Wisdom is not necessarily knowledge; knowledge is certainly not necessarily wisdom. People can have extraordinary knowledge but sorely lack wisdom. Wisdom is the way you *use* or *apply* the knowledge you have. Knowledge may be a storage of facts or information. Some people know many facts; some have a lot of information. Could this be the right understanding of an utterance of knowledge? Possibly. God could in a moment of need call on such a person to give a timely word based upon years of study.

We should connect all these gifts with the concept of common grace—special grace in nature. All of humankind have a level of common grace. It is called common not because it is ordinary but because it is given commonly to all—whether or not you get saved. Common grace refers to the natural abilities you received in the way God made you, whether or not you become a Christian. At the level of common grace is your intelligence, your capacity to acquire and retain knowledge, your memory, and the genetic tendencies you inherited from your parents.

It is my observation that gifts of the Spirit sometimes connect to one's natural abilities. For example, once redeemed through salvation in Christ, people who have natural shrewdness or good judgment are likely to have the gift of wisdom. In other words, if a naturally clever person becomes a Christian, it should not be surprising that he or she has the gift of the utterance of wisdom. It is the same with the gift of the utterance of knowledge.

The word *knowledge* comes from *gnosis*—sometimes referring to revealed knowledge, vis-à-vis *oida*, which generally means knowledge of facts.[2] *Gnosis* would fit well with the way Charismatics often use the term *word of knowledge*. The Spirit sometimes reveals words of knowledge to them.

Could an utterance of knowledge refer to a person's intellect and wealth of knowledge? Possibly. A person highly learned but filled with the Spirit may have a message of knowledge based upon what he or she has accumulated over the years. This would also show how common grace figures in the gifts. A person with a vast knowledge of the Bible might also deliver an utterance of knowledge—whether on a one-to-one basis or from a pulpit to many.

The gift of faith can be puzzling. If we are justified—saved—by faith, why would Paul list faith as a gift of the Spirit?

There are two kinds of faith, generally speaking. First, there is saving faith. This kind of faith justifies; it redeems. This faith assures you of a home in Heaven when you die. It comes by transferring the trust you once had in your good works to what Jesus did for you by His death. It is when you believe you are saved through Christ alone.

Second, there is persistent faith. This faith leads to your inheritance. All Christians are called to come into their inheritance. Some do; some don't. Those who do will not only come into an inheritance in this life but also receive a reward at the judgment seat of Christ (1 Cor. 3:14; 2 Cor. 5:10). Those who do not persist in faith not only blow away the inheritance they could have had on earth but will forfeit a reward at the judgment seat of Christ (1 Cor. 3:15).

Those described in Hebrews 11 are men and women with persistent faith. Hebrews 11 is not about saving faith; it is about people who persevered and accomplished great things for God—those "of whom the world was not worthy" (v. 38).

Which type of faith does Paul list with the gifts of the Spirit? It is not saving faith; he is writing to Christians who are already saved. It certainly could be persistent faith such as the faith that described Abraham, Isaac, Jacob, Joseph, Moses, and others.

I believe there may be a third category for this faith given as a gift of the Spirit—a faith given for a special circumstance or a particular situation. You might receive faith that someone you are praying for will get saved. You might receive faith for answered prayer: "If we know that he hears us in whatever we ask, we know that we have the requests that we have asked of him" (1 John 5:15). That is a big "if"—knowing that the Most High has heard us. But God may grant this faith for a special occasion to you. The gift of faith is probably best understood as special faith for a particular occasion.

PERSONAL REFLECTION

Spend some time with Jesus, asking Him to reveal to you some of the unique ways that you were made. What special gifts, talents, and abilities were woven into your personality when God dreamed you up? How do you see that common grace acting in your life?

_____

_____

_____

Have you ever experienced a moment of supernatural wisdom, a word of knowledge, or a sudden increase in your faith for a particular situation? What was the event, and how did the manifestation of that spiritual gift impact you and those around you?

_____

_____

_____

THE GIFTS OF HEALING, MIRACLES, PROPHECY, AND DISTINGUISHING SPIRITS

Never doubt God's mighty power to work in you and accomplish all this. He will achieve infinitely more than your greatest request, your most unbelievable dream, and exceed your wildest imagination! He will outdo them all, for his miraculous power constantly energizes you. Now we offer up to God all the glorious praise that rises from every church in every generation through Jesus Christ—and all that will yet be manifest through time and eternity. Amen!

—EPHESIANS 3:20–21, TPT

ALL OF US could certainly wish for the spiritual gift of healing. A few years ago, my wife, Louise, needed a second operation on her back for a herniated disc. The pain she experienced was the worst of our sixty years of marriage. I prayed for her dozens and dozens and dozens of times. No healing.

However, on a different occasion, I put my hands on the temples of a Scottish woman whom I had never met and prayed for her at her request. She wrote months later to say she had sinus headaches for five years, but that day I prayed for her was the worst of her life. "When you prayed, I felt nothing," she wrote. "But a few hours later I realized the pain was gone and never came back." Does that mean I have the gift of healing? No. I didn't even have faith for her healing! I too felt nothing. I was in a hurry. I stopped to pray for her out of courtesy, but God overruled my lack of faith and healed this woman.

Perhaps you see by now that there is an element of mystery in the gifts of the Spirit. I don't fully understand any of them! We can only do our best to grasp what the Holy Spirit is teaching. I have learned this much: *don't try to figure God out.*

Do some people have a permanent gift of healing? Possibly. Oral Roberts (1918–2009), whom I met three times in his house in California, came the closest to anybody I know of who had this gift. There are no doubt thousands of people with little or no profile who have—at least at times—a gift of healing. It is a mystery.

The gift of working of miracles is equally mysterious. Does this refer to healing or a sudden miracle of a rather spectacular nature, such as a person delivered of demon possession? My friend Charles Carrin tells of a time when a dangerous storm front—potentially a tornado—was headed for Florence, Alabama, while he was preaching in a service there. He led the congregation in praying and taking authority, commanding the storm to bypass the city. After Charles and the people prayed, the storm split—half of it went to the south, half to the north—and completely avoided Florence. The split storm then came back together on the other side of the city.[1] This activity appeared on the radar screen, and people there still talk about it.

That event surely qualifies as a miracle. Sometimes healings are also called miracles. Supernatural healings are miracles, but not all miracles are healings.

Paul especially wanted the Corinthians to have the gift of prophecy. "Pursue love, and earnestly desire the spiritual gifts, especially that you may prophesy" (1 Cor. 14:1). The gift of prophecy is the ability to unveil God's will for the church at a given moment. It is not an invitation to be another Elijah, Isaiah, or Jeremiah. The apostles were successors to these major men in the Old Testament.

The gift of prophecy in the New Testament was for the local church. When people came together to worship, some people would offer a prophetic word that edified the body of Christ. The Corinthians made the mistake—often repeated today—of thinking speaking in tongues was everything. The Corinthians relished their speaking in tongues, which no one understood. Paul rebuked them soundly, stating: "I would rather speak five words with my mind in order to instruct others, than ten thousand words in a tongue" (1 Cor. 14:19).

We must test any prophetic word. "Do not despise prophecies, but test everything; hold fast what is good" (1 Thess. 5:20–21).

There were often hard times when we were at Westminster Chapel. One situation had to do with our family; certain people in the church had been cruel regarding one of our children. One Sunday morning Louise went to the chapel with a very heavy heart. As soon as she arrived, a Nigerian woman named Grace, who had been waiting for Louise, came to her with a prophetic word. She said *one single word* to Louise, a word Louise knew immediately was from the Lord. It gave her tremendous comfort.

That is an example of the gift of prophecy in the church.

After prophecy, Paul lists the gift of the ability to distinguish between spirits. To distinguish between spirits means primarily to know the difference between the Holy Spirit and a demonic spirit.

It is a timely reminder that we are in a war with Satan. He hates Jesus Christ, who is his prime enemy, and also those who are *in* Christ. Satan has our numbers and will do *anything* to shake us, divert us, deceive us, or oppress us. It is important therefore to know the enemy. However, you must know the real thing before you can recognize the counterfeit.

This gift is valuable. We need to be able to see what is real and genuine and what is not. The first task, then, is to be able to recognize the true Holy Spirit. He is the true Spirit of God, the third person of the Trinity. I think many sincere Christians immediately and hastily focus on the demonic when applying this particular gift of the Spirit. Do not make this mistake. Our first responsibility is to be able to know and discern the *true presence of God*. As I said, we must know the *real* before we can recognize the counterfeit. It is a big mistake to focus on the counterfeit and become an expert in demonology. I have known people who thrive on books about the occult, witchcraft, and demons. Such people always strike me as not being very spiritual or godly.

John said we must "test the spirits to see whether they are from God" (1 John 4:1). He gave this instruction because there are false prophets around. "Every spirit that confesses that Jesus Christ has come in the flesh is from God" (v. 2). When I was asked to give my opinion of the Toronto Blessing, a revival that took place at the Toronto Airport Vineyard back in 1994, I began with 1 John 4:1–4. As I will show further later, it became obvious to me that what was abroad in the Toronto church was the true Holy Spirit; the people there, from John Arnott to the leadership, passed this test.

You might be asking, "But, R. T., could there not be much of the flesh in such a move of God?" Yes. Even if one discerns that the Holy Spirit is truly at work, one can expect the flesh to be present. It always is—as in the case of the Great Awakening of the eighteenth century. Even George Whitefield (1714–1770), one of the primary leaders in this move of the Spirit, sadly did things that were of the flesh.

These things said, the first task is to know how to discern the Holy Spirit of God. If one has the ability to recognize the Holy Spirit, it becomes relatively easy to discern the demonic. The contrast will be obvious. However, if you *begin* with trying to spot the demonic, you may miss seeing what is going on. You must begin with a solid and sound understanding of the person and presence of the Holy Spirit. Then the demonic—if present—will saliently manifest.

PERSONAL REFLECTION

Recall any stories from the Bible you can that depict the gift of healing, miracles, prophecy, or discerning spirits. Make a note of any details that stand out to you. What precipitated the movement of the Spirit in this way? What was the effect on the people who witnessed it?

_____

_____

_____

Do some spiritual gifts feel foreign or uncomfortable to you? Spend some time with the Lord, asking Him for His perspective on those gifts. Why does He want us to pursue them? What stands in the way of our pursuit of His gifts?

THE GIFT OF TONGUES AND THEIR INTERPRETATION

And these signs will accompany those who believe: in my name
they will cast out demons; they will speak in new tongues.
—MARK 16:17

TONGUE, MEANING "LANGUAGE," is a translation of the Greek *glōssa*.[1] The modern Charismatic movement began in the 1960s. As I will show further later, it was initially known as the glossolalia movement, owing to the emphasis on speaking in tongues.

Until 1960 it was primarily Pentecostals, having their origin in the Azusa Street Revival in Los Angeles (1906), who were associated with speaking in tongues. They were mainly found in the Elim Pentecostal Church (a United Kingdom–based denomination), the Assemblies of God, the Pentecostal Holiness Church, the Church of God, and the Church of God of Prophecy.

The Charismatic movement, as it is named, began decades later when a growing number of churches in mainline denominations suddenly encountered and embraced what were thought of as Pentecostal experiences. The new movement included Episcopalians, Baptists, Presbyterians, Reformed, and others— including Roman Catholics. The word *charismatic* comes from the Greek *charisma*—meaning "grace-gift."[2] As the name indicates, *all* gifts of the Spirit—not merely tongues—were given recognition in the new movement.

The gift of "various kinds of tongues," then, means different languages (1 Cor. 12:10). The inauguration of this gift came on the day of Pentecost when 120 disciples were filled with the Spirit and "began to speak in other tongues as the Spirit gave them utterance" (Acts 2:4). They were baptized with the Holy Spirit as Jesus had announced: "You will be baptized with the Holy Spirit not many days from now" (1:5).

For this reason, most Pentecostals and Charismatics hold that you will speak with tongues if you are baptized with the Spirit and that if you don't speak with tongues, you have not been baptized with the Spirit. But not all of us agree with this. I am convinced that what happened to me on October 31, 1955, was the baptism of the Holy Spirit. Some four months later, I spoke in tongues, however. I say more about this in *Holy Fire*.

That said, the 120 disciples spoke with "other tongues"—languages not their own. Moreover, people from foreign nations *heard* the disciples speaking in *their* languages. "Each one was hearing them speak in his own language" (Acts 2:6). It was a double miracle: they spoke in other tongues and were heard by foreigners in their own languages!

There has been much discussion about whether a person who receives a "heavenly language" experiences exactly what happened to the 120 on the day of Pentecost. Some say yes; some say no. I lean to the latter because the heavenly language is almost always a case of speaking unintelligible sounds that no one understands. Although the tongues phenomenon certainly began at Pentecost, it would not seem that praying in the

Spirit—when one "speaks not to men but to God"—is the same thing; "for no one understands him, but he utters mysteries in the Spirit" (1 Cor. 14:2).

This is why Paul speaks of "various kinds of tongues." I see at least three possibilities: (1) one speaks in some *known* language— at least known to some people somewhere on the planet; (2) it is a unique language—no one understands the person, which is what 1 Corinthians 14:2 refers to; or (3) it is an angelic language— literally the untranslated tongue of angels. This could be why Paul refers to "the tongues of men and of angels" (1 Cor. 13:1).

Finally, the gift of the interpretation of tongues implies that there *is* an interpretation of any tongue uttered by the power of the Holy Spirit. In other words, speaking or praying in tongues is not meaningless. Some people are enabled by the Spirit to speak in various tongues; others are able to interpret what they said. Paul admonished the Corinthians not to speak in tongues in a gathering where visitors would have no clue what was said. If one does speak in tongues publicly, it is fine—that is, as long as someone has the interpretation.

The problem often encountered is when people give their *own* interpretation of the message in tongues that they them-selves just uttered. This may seem benign, but it is suspect. It was not what Paul had in mind. He wanted someone who had the gift of interpretation to step in and interpret. When the same person gives the interpretation, it lacks credibility and authenticity.

Pastor Jack Hayford tells the story of being on a plane when he felt led to utter a tongue to the person sitting next to him. He dreaded doing it and tried to avoid it, but it was on him so strongly that he gave in and uttered a strange set of syllables he did not understand. However, the man next to him was a Native American and turned to Jack to say, "You have just said words that only my tribe speaks!" It was a wonderful testimony.[3] There are many stories like this where a person spoke in a language he or she did not understand, but others were astonished to recognize their own language!

Once, when we were living in Key Largo, Florida, I sat on the porch overlooking Largo Sound, and the following happened to me. I was praying and uttered a tongue when I immediately heard these words: "Stop taking yourself so seriously." I am sure it was an instantaneous interpretation—and a loving rebuke that I needed.

The gift of interpretation of tongues is, I think, rare. For that matter, perhaps all the genuine gifts of the Spirit are rare these days. I am no cessationist. However, I think we give our critics credibility when we tolerate the counterfeit without testing all things. I fear that some of us are so anxious to see God work that we try to *make* things happen—whether trying to prove that someone is healed when he or she is not healed or uttering prophecies that never come true.

The greatest freedom is having nothing to prove.

PERSONAL REFLECTION

Have you been baptized in the Spirit? Did you receive the gift of tongues? If so, how does operating in that gift edify you?

_____

_____

_____

If you don't speak in tongues, is that one of the gifts you would like to eagerly pursue? What interpretations of tongues have you heard? How did hearing the interpretation impact you?

_____

_____

_____

THE SPIRIT OF TRUTH

God is Spirit, and those who worship Him
must worship in spirit and truth.
—JOHN 4:24, NKJV

A. W. TOZER (1897–1963) is credited with these words: "It is never possible to have the Spirit without at least some measure of truth."[1] This is because the Holy Spirit is the "Spirit *of truth*, who proceeds from the Father" (John 15:26, emphasis added). There is a sense in which the essence of God is *truth*.

To me, the *truth about* God and the truth *of* God and the truth *from* God are among the most dazzling, breathtaking, and thrilling things about God. This is why He has "magnified" His Word above all His name (Ps. 138:2, KJV)! His Word is truth. Jesus prayed, "Sanctify them in the truth; your word is truth" (John 17:17).

The Welsh Revival was one of the great moves of the Holy Spirit in modern church history. Estimates of the number of people converted are as high as one hundred thousand.[2] The pubs and jails emptied. Bethan Phillips was a six-year-old living in London when her father took her and her older brother out of school and put them on a train to their grandparents' home in

Wales. Members of the family criticized him for taking the two children out of school. His reply: "They can go to school any-time, but perhaps they may never again see revival."[3]

Bethan grew up and married Dr. Martyn Lloyd-Jones. Years later, in her eighties, she spoke with me about that time, recalling when she personally witnessed the Welsh Revival. Dr. Lloyd-Jones also told me this story:

> A coal miner came home from work, and his wife had not cooked his dinner. She had gone to the church to be in the revival. He was so livid and upset that he decided to go to the church and stop the revival. When he arrived, he could not get into the building as people were crowding the door. Refusing to be kept out, he angrily elbowed his way through the people into the church. The next thing he remembers is being on his knees in front of the pulpit, crying to God for mercy! Those who wit-nessed the event said that he managed to get inside the church and literally stepped on the top of the back pew, then made his way to the front by stepping on the top of every pew. He then fell before the pulpit and began praying.

Serious critics of the Welsh Revival said this phenomenon could not be of God because of the absence of preaching. I reply: What exactly did they sing during that epochal era? If it were a false spirit but not the Holy Spirit, one would expect that the hymns would be strange, heretical, and unbiblical. This was not the case! They sang the biblical hymns of the church!

Think about this. What if the God who exists were an untruthful God? What if He lied? What if He could not be believed? What if He were not faithful? He did not say, "I will turn myself into a God of truth." He did not say, "I will be truthful." Nor did He say, "I will always tell the truth." No. He *is* truth. It is impossible for Him not to be truthful. The everlasting God *is a God of truth*. He is a God of honesty and integrity. He is a God who is faithful and keeps His Word! You can fully trust Him.

This easily brings me to tears. What a wonderful God we have! How blessed can we be? It doesn't get better than this.

Therefore, if one begins in the Spirit, it is because *truth* was present. However, the Galatians sadly wandered from the truth. Not totally. Even in their weakened condition, they had a measure of truth. The issue? The Gospel. It often is. Paul was alarmed at what was happening to his converts at Galatia. He corresponded with deepest urgency: "I am astonished that you are so quickly deserting him who called you in the grace of Christ and are turning to a different gospel—not that there is another one, but there are some who trouble you and want to distort the gospel of Christ" (Gal. 1:6–7).

It is worth noting that Paul does not question their conversions. There might be some today who would say that if the Galatians' conversions were genuine, they would not have been so quickly influenced by false teaching. Quite the contrary; Paul does all he can to sort them out lest they be demoralized and disillusioned. The reason for Paul's letters, which form almost a third of the New Testament, is because all converts need teaching and often warning.

Like many churches today throughout the world, the Galatians had the Spirit but only a measure of truth, to refer to Tozer's comment. There is no reason to believe that they abandoned the essentials of the faith such as Jesus' deity and humanity and His bodily resurrection and ascension. As long as one believes in Jesus as the God-man and His resurrection from the dead, he or she is saved (Rom. 10:9–10). Even if you say "saved but only just," I would agree, but saved the Galatians were, and that is the essential truth we must not forget.

This explains how a church—or a minister—can have the Holy Spirit but lack in sound theology. Indeed, with the Holy Spirit, people can do extraordinary things—for example, preach impressive sermons, write good music and poetry, or be instruments in healing, lively worship, true deliverances, and remarkable prophecies. What is more, as we have seen, the gifts of the Spirit are irrevocable (Rom. 11:29), meaning that (1) you do not lose them and (2) personal holiness does not guarantee they will be granted. The anointing comes by the sovereign will of God.

Never forget that King Saul prophesied on his way to kill David (1 Sam. 19:24). When God says, "I . . . will show mercy on whom I will show mercy" (Exod. 33:19; see also Romans 9:15), this means that He withholds judgment on those of us who deserve judgment. The difference between grace and mercy is this: grace is receiving favor we *don't* deserve; mercy is having God withhold justice we *do* deserve.

This also means God has mercy on those who are not always theologically correct. This lesson teaches those of us who wrongly assume that our sound theology scores points with God. God might choose to bypass those of us who fancy ourselves to be sound in doctrine, and He might bless those who—at the moment—may not have a great measure of truth!

PERSONAL REFLECTION

Have you encountered the Holy Spirit without anyone preaching? How did you experience the truth of God through that encounter?

_____

_____

_____

What does it mean to you to know that God is truth and that He is absolutely trustworthy? Think of an area of your life where you could use the reminder of His faithfulness. Spend some time thanking God for who He is as His Spirit leads you into all truth.

_____

_____

_____

A WIDER NET

But when the truth-giving Spirit comes, he will unveil
the reality of every truth within you. He won't speak his
own message, but only what he hears from the Father, and
he will reveal prophetically to you what is to come.
—JOHN 16:13, TPT

ONE DAY IN 1994, I received a phone call from Ken Costa, churchwarden of Holy Trinity Brompton (HTB), a prominent Anglican church in London (now the largest in England) also known to be open to the Holy Spirit. Ken said to me, "Some unusual things are happening in our church, and I am wondering if you have any sermons on 1 John 4:1–4?" Yes. I immediately sent him four sermons on those verses that deal with testing the spirits to see whether they are of God. After Ken read those sermons, he asked to take me to lunch to talk about what was going on at HTB. I went to lunch to warn him. Several days before, I had heard about people being prayed for and falling down with laughter. People said this came from Toronto. I initially doubted that such was of God. I certainly didn't want to think it was of God. I found that sort of thing disturbing!

Also, if I am totally candid, I felt a little bit betrayed by God. After all, if what was going on at HTB was indeed from the Holy

Spirit, if it was genuinely of God, it would surely have come to Westminster Chapel first! I struggled to believe that He would bless HTB and not Westminster Chapel!

I considered the Church of England apostate. "Surely God would not bless a church with all those Etonians on their staff," I thought, "with their posh Sloane Square accents!" We at Westminster Chapel were ordinary Christians as described in 1 Corinthians 1:26–31. Jealousy is a hard sin to see in ourselves.

There was more. I had faithfully upheld the historic Gospel against severe opposition and had become vulnerable by having Arthur Blessitt turn us upside down. Furthermore, our church had days of prayer and fasting. I was out on the streets witnessing to the lost. I am ashamed to say that I assumed that God would surely favor us over Anglican churches, including HTB.

Ken had not come to persuade me of what was going on in his church. He sincerely wanted my opinion. But halfway through that lunch, I became extremely concerned that, just maybe, I was opposing a work of God merely because it did not come to us first. I recalled how many Christians opposed the Welsh Revival. I knew there was a very long tradition that resisted what God was doing in certain generations. I truly began to fear that I might be on the wrong side.

There was also a glow on Ken's face that began to give me pause. Not only that, but HTB clearly passed the test of 1 John 4:1–4. They may or may not have been as Reformed as I was, but neither was John Wesley!

By the time we finished lunch, I was sobered from head to toe. I phoned Louise to tell her I believed I had been wrong with regard to the Toronto Blessing. I called my deacons together to say the same thing. To their credit, they stood with me. I had warned my congregation at Westminster weeks before of what was going on at HTB, but after that lunch with Ken, I publicly took it back. I am so glad I did.

Later that year my wife, Louise, was miraculously healed in seconds through a man who is known to be the "father" of the Toronto Blessing. Louise came into the chapel vestry that Saturday morning, having slept little the night before. She admits that she had no faith but was willing to let "that man" (she did not know who he was) pray for her. She was instantly healed. I can pick that man's theology to pieces! He became a dear friend and will vouch for how I have pleaded with him to get sorted out on certain issues. I still pray that he will come around. I could refer to many others who see miracles but are not what I personally regard as sound. There are those whose theology (surely) must make the angels blush but whom God uses amazingly.

When God said, "I will have mercy on whom I have mercy" (Rom. 9:15), He meant just that. He is sovereign and shows mercy to whom He will—whether to a church or an individual. Why? Because that is the way He is.

The God of the Bible is a God of truth. The truth is, He sometimes blesses those that you and I would never choose. He bypasses those that you and I would assume to be exactly where God would manifest His glory next.

God has a wider net than some of us to pull in those He chooses to bless. The presence of the Holy Spirit—the Spirit of truth—can manifest in amazing ways, indeed manifesting *in* those and to those you and I might think have but a small measure of truth. Paul did not give up on the Galatians. We must not give up on one another who sincerely and earnestly seek the honor and glory of God.

PERSONAL REFLECTION

Have you experienced seeing someone else receive the blessing that you were praying and waiting for? What was that experience like for you? If you were offended, how did you recover from that?

_____

_____

_____

If you have experienced a move of God's Holy Spirit, what was the most challenging thing about that atmosphere for you? Is there a preacher or spiritual leader who currently offends you? Take some time to hear God's heart for that leader and return the seat of judgment back to God.

_____

_____

_____

HIS WORD ABOVE HIS NAME

Thou hast magnified thy word above all thy name.
—PSALM 138:2, KJV

WHEN YOU THINK how God wants His name to be honored, think about this: He magnifies His Word above all His name. Knowing that modern translations strangely gloss over this verse—interpreting rather than translating—I began to wonder if maybe the King James Version got it wrong, although the English Standard Version has a footnote: "You have exalted your word above all your name." I asked the late Dr. Michael Eaton (1942–2017), one of the most learned men I have ever known—who knew his Hebrew—to tell me the truth about Psalm 138:2. He assured me that the Hebrew is to be literally translated "You have magnified Your word above all Your name."

To be doubly sure, I contacted my friend Rabbi Sir David Rosen, an erudite Orthodox Jew in Jerusalem. Here is what he wrote to me: "The translation should be, 'You have exalted Your word (or Your speech) above Your Name,' i.e., the Divine Word is more important to Him than His Name." David added that *word* referred to the Torah—God's commands. Amazing.

I take *Word* to refer to Holy Scripture—the Bible. I don't think this fundamental if not elementary point can be made too often. In other words, when I refer to Word and Spirit, I mean the Bible and the Holy Spirit.

It should be noted, however, that two Greek words are translated as "word" in English: *logos* and *rhema*. Since these words are interchangeable, one must not press any hoped-for distinction too far. That said, generally speaking—and for the purpose of this book—I choose to make *logos* refer to the Word of God in *print*. I say this because *logos* also refers to the Word of God in *person*: "In the beginning was the Word . . .and the Word became flesh" (John 1:1, 14).

Furthermore, Paul's last word to Timothy included this command: "Preach the word [*logos*]" (2 Tim. 4:2). Could Paul have used *rhema* instead of *logos* in 2 Timothy 4:2? Yes, he could have used either. Again and again, they come to the same meaning.

The Greek word *logos* and words that spring from it are used more than three hundred times in the New Testament. *Rhema* is used about seventy times. Some have wanted to show that *logos* is a stronger word—that only *logos* refers to Scripture. However, that view won't hold up. For example, when Jesus quoted Deuteronomy 8:3, "Man shall not live by bread alone, but by every *word* that comes from the mouth of God," *rhema* is used by Matthew (4:4, emphasis added). This alone shows that *rhema* can be used to mean Scripture as well as *logos*.

Because *rhema* and *logos* can be used interchangeably, there are those who hastily conclude that a prophetic word—which they want to call a "rhema word"—is equal to Scripture. Really?

I reply: Never. Never. Never. Never. Never. To do this is dangerous and will encourage people to trivialize Holy Scripture. That is what Satan wants.

Regardless of the stature or reputation of the person giving it, never accept a prophetic word given to you as equal to Holy Scripture—even if the prophetic word turns out to be true. The fact that a prophetic word turns out to be true still does not give it canonical status. There are levels of authority; only Holy Scripture should be seen as the infallible Word of God.

I myself hope for and pray for a "rhema word" virtually every time I read the Bible, whether in my daily reading or when I preach. Yes, when I preach, I hope God will speak to me afresh and show me things I have not thought of before. I would define the "rhema word" I am seeking as when God's Word becomes very, very direct and very, very real—when it is unquestionably genuine and true. It can happen when I am very discouraged. It can happen when I need clear guidance. It can happen when I am routinely going through my Bible reading plan. It might happen when I least expect it.

In June 1970 at a Southern Baptist Convention, I was high up in the balcony listening to a sermon but pleading with the Lord to know the next step forward. The issue: Should I finish my education or stay where I was at the time—pastor of Lauderdale Manors Baptist Church in Fort Lauderdale, Florida? We were happy there. Nothing was wrong; all was good—except my growing frustration that I would eventually be sorry if I did not pursue further education through a seminary.

I knew that even if I gave up my church, it would take at least five years to complete what I always wanted to do—get a degree from a British university. "But," I said to myself, "I will be forty years old by then. What is more, I know the Gospel. I know my Bible. What can I learn at seminary?"

Although I tried to talk myself out of going, I felt an underlying persuasion that I should do it *now* or regret it for the rest of my life. "How will I feel when I am forty years old? Will I be glad then that I did it? Yes. However, is this the Lord talking to me, or is it me talking to myself?"

I reached for my little New Testament I always carried with me. I had a deep-seated feeling that God was about to speak. My heart pounded as I held my New Testament in my hand. Then I prayed, "Lord, if You are going to speak, please let the word be objective—a word that stands on its own, not merely a 'Thus says the Lord, I am with you' sort of word."

I opened my New Testament, and my eyes fell on these words: "And Moses was learned in all the wisdom of the Egyptians, and was mighty in words and in deeds. And when he was full forty years old, it came into his heart to visit his brethren the children of Israel" (Acts 7:22–23, KJV). That did it for me. I turned to Louise and said, "We will resign Lauderdale Manors this Sunday. We're moving for me to finish my education."

I never looked back. That is one of the clearest words from the Lord I ever received. It answered two things that gripped me: (1) Why go to seminary when I know the Bible? Answer: Moses was learned in the wisdom of the Egyptians; it was part of his preparation. (2) The age forty was a huge factor; Moses was forty when God really began to prepare him—that is, to launch him into the primary calling or purpose for his life.

In other words, I believe that God can speak like this. He can use the Bible; He can use a person with a prophetic word.

PERSONAL REFLECTION

Think back to a time when you experienced a passage of Scripture becoming very direct and real to you in a new way.

What was the passage? How did that "rhema word" teach, guide, or encourage you?

_____

_____

_____

Have you ever felt a tug from the Holy Spirit to do something that you couldn't ignore? How did the Lord confirm His word to you? How did following His guidance impact your life?

_____

_____

_____

As Much of God as We Can Get

O God, You are my God;
with deepest longing I will seek You;
My soul [my life, my very self] thirsts for You,
my flesh longs and sighs for You,
In a dry and weary land where there is no water.
—Psalm 63:1, AMP

CESSATIONISTS (THOSE WHO believe that the gifts of the Spirit ceased long ago) hold only to a soteriological doctrine of the Spirit. This doctrine claims that the Holy Spirit works only to *apply the preaching* of the Gospel. The word *soteriology* refers to salvation. Cessationists do not believe that the Holy Spirit can work immediately and directly in the human heart as He did in the Book of Acts. They believe the Holy Spirit gets involved in the preaching of the Gospel and applies the Word in human hearts so that people become convicted of sin, righteousness, and judgment to come. These people are, of course, right to believe that the Holy Spirit works in this way. But they are wrong to think that the Holy Spirit works *only* in this manner.

It is important for one's doctrine of assurance to know you are saved. There are two levels of assurance: syllogistic reasoning and the "immediate and direct"[1] witness of the Holy Spirit. The former is also called the indirect or mediate witness of the Holy Spirit. For example:

All who believe in Jesus are saved.

I believe in Jesus.

Therefore, I am saved.

What is wrong with that kind of reasoning? Nothing. It is absolutely right. It is the Holy Spirit who applies the Gospel and leads people to trust Jesus Christ alone for their salvation. It is not that they necessarily *feel* anything; it is an intellectual process. It is cerebral. It is reasoning. The English Puritans—especially William Perkins (1558–1602)—knew it as a "practical syllogism." Many if not most people come to initial assurance of salvation this way.

They are quite right to say, "I know I am saved because Jesus died for me on the cross." However, there is a higher level of assurance.

That is the "direct, immediate" witness of the Holy Spirit. I learned this phrase from Dr. Lloyd-Jones.[2] The practical syllogism is not immediate and direct; it is *mediated to us by reasoning*. It is sound reasoning. It is safe and secure. But there is such a thing as an immediate and direct witness of the Spirit. It is as though it bypasses the mind. It is when the Holy Spirit testifies to the *heart*. It is the most amazing feeling.

What is more, this type of assurance is so powerful that one does not actually *need* reasoning to be sure that he or she is saved! The Holy Spirit Himself tells you that you are a child of God. Dr. Lloyd-Jones always called it "the highest form of assurance."[3]

This kind of experience was typical with the original Methodists. They believed that when a person became a

Christian, he or she *felt* something! They *knew* that they were born again by the direct witness of the Holy Spirit. It was a conscious experience. There are two points of view on this. Some believe this immediate and direct witness of the Spirit comes at conversion.

I believe this immediate and direct witness of the Spirit more often comes to those who have *already been converted*. It happens when people want *more* than the Holy Spirit applying the Gospel via a practical syllogism.

My friend Charles Carrin, who became a Primitive Baptist pastor, tells how he wanted more than what he experienced at conversion—real though that was. He asked his brother, "Is there not more?"

His brother replied, "No, Charles, you got it all at conversion."

Years later, having been in the ministry for a good number of years, he was invited to be a chaplain at a federal penitentiary in Atlanta and assigned to an inmate who had been miraculously converted while in prison. This prisoner also had received the immediate witness of the Spirit along with certain gifts of the Spirit. Charles was supposed to provide spiritual help, but instead, Charles began to realize that he *needed* spiritual help! After a while Charles experienced the immediate and direct witness of the Holy Spirit. His Baptist church subsequently threw him out![4]

Why should a person disdain the idea of wanting more? Why are some threatened by the idea of more? I suspect that when told they "got it all at conversion," some are relieved of the need to press on for more of God. They feel they can sit back, stay in their comfort zones, and refuse to be bothered by the idea that there is anything more after conversion.

This is not so. You and I should surely want as much of God as we can get.

Personal Reflection

Do you remember when you first came into a relationship with Jesus? How did you know you were saved? Did you feel anything? Which resonates more with your experience: syllogistic reasoning or the immediate and direct witness of the Holy Spirit?

_____

_____

_____

How have you experienced the Holy Spirit move in your own life? Do you believe that there is more of God available to you?

_____

_____

_____

THE GOSPEL OF POWER

Since we have now been justified by his blood, how much
more shall we be saved from God's wrath through him!
—ROMANS 5:9, NIV

WHY BE A Christian? This question is of utmost importance. Do you have an answer? Some would say, "You should be a Christian because you will be a happier person." Really? The first person I baptized in London was a Los Angeles Jewish businessman who was converted one Sunday evening at Westminster Chapel. We later became friends, even spent parts of holidays together. He was wonderfully converted, but he said to me one day, "Before I became a Christian, I was a happy man." He wasn't complaining; he was admitting that being a Christian was costly—and sometimes painful. None of his family or his friends became Christians.

Some might answer this question, "You should become a Christian because it could help your marriage." Really? Divorce rates might prove otherwise. I have found that marriages are helped when couples put Jesus Christ first in their lives; they not only are faithful to each other but also stop pointing the finger and mutually forgive each other for their faults.

The reason a person should be a Christian, says Paul, is

because of the wrath of God (Rom. 1:18; 5:9; 1 Thess. 1:10). Most Christians can quote John 3:16: "For God so loved the world that he gave his one and only Son, that whoever believes in him shall *not perish* [meaning that they will *not go to Hell*] but have eternal life" (NIV, emphasis added). Once a person is a Christian, he or she becomes a part of the body of Christ—the church. God wants the church to be the salt of the earth. We become salt and light when we uphold the Scriptures and manifest the power of God with equal force. The last thing we want is for these two to be separated, and yet they have been.

I believe God hates this divorce between His Spirit and His Word as much as He hates the divorce of a husband and wife (Mal. 2:16, NLT; see footnote in ESV)—even more so, if that is possible.

It was a silent divorce. It is impossible to know precisely when it took place. It may have happened many times in the course of church history. Sometime before AD 65, Paul wrote of a future "rebellion" (2 Thess. 2:3). The King James Version calls it "a falling away." Between AD 90 and 100, Jesus, speaking from the right hand of God in Heaven, said that the church of Ephesus had "abandoned the love you had at first" (Rev. 2:4). What was their first love? The Gospel. Read the Book of Ephesians alongside Acts 19 and 20. The Gospel was paramount at Ephesus. So too was the evidence of power.

What is more, when you read the earliest writings of the apostolic fathers (people such as Ignatius and Polycarp from the second and third centuries)—as I show in *Whatever Happened to the Gospel?*—the Gospel appears to have been replaced by moralism and emphasis on good works. The Gospel is the "power of God for salvation" (Rom. 1:16). But

Paul said that in the last days there would be people "having the appearance of godliness, but denying its power" (2 Tim. 3:5). That is the Word without the Spirit.

It is a gospel sometimes upheld by cerebral teaching that intentionally rejects the gifts of the Spirit. Often it is good, sound doctrine, but it lacks power. Paul calls this quenching the Spirit or putting out the Spirit's fire (1 Thess. 5:19; cf. TPT). An example of this is cessationist teaching, as I show in *Holy Fire*. Such teaching—which has utterly no foundation in Scripture—quenches the Spirit before the Spirit is allowed to manifest His power.

At the original Word and Spirit Conference in October 1992, I first expressed my view that there has been a silent divorce in the church, generally speaking, between the Word and the Spirit. When there is a divorce, sometimes the children stay with the mother; sometimes with the father. In the divorce between the Word and the Spirit, you have those on the Word side and those on the Spirit side.

PERSONAL REFLECTION

In what ways have you experienced the cost of becoming a Christian? In what ways have you experienced the blessings of your relationship with God?

_____

_____

_____

How have you experienced the evidence of God's power in your own life? Have you seen the full Gospel get watered down into moralism or an emphasis on good works? How has the silent divorce between the Word and the Spirit impacted you?

_____

_____

_____

WAKING UP THE CHURCH

Jesus replied, "Your mistake is that you don't know the
Scriptures, and you don't know the power of God."
—MATTHEW 22:29, NLT

TAKE FOR EXAMPLE those on the Word side. Their message is that we must get back to the Bible, earnestly contend for the faith once delivered to the saints (Jude 3),
get back to Reformation doctrine (justification by faith as taught
by Martin Luther), rediscover assurance of salvation as taught
by John Calvin, and return to the teaching of the sovereignty of
God as preached by Jonathan Edwards.

What is wrong with this emphasis? Nothing, in my opinion;
it is exactly right.

Take those on the Spirit side. Their message is that we must
get back to the Book of Acts where there were signs, wonders,
and miracles—gifts of the Spirit in operation. When they had
a prayer meeting, the place was "shaken" (Acts 4:31). Get into
Peter's "shadow," and you were healed (5:15); lie to the Holy
Spirit and you were struck dead on the spot (5:1–10).

What is wrong with this emphasis? Nothing, in my opinion;
it is exactly right.

The problem is that neither will learn from the other; they talk past each other and don't take the other point of view seriously.

According to Jesus in Matthew 22:29, the Sadducees were ignorant of two things: the Scriptures and the power of God. Remember, the Scriptures refer to the Bible (the Word); the power of God, to the Holy Spirit (the Spirit).

In the case of the Sadducees, they had only the Old Testament scriptures, of course. Jesus was saying they were ignorant of the Old Testament. We have the New Testament, which they did not have. Never forget that the New Testament is as infallible and God-breathed as the Old Testament. They have equal status as the Word of God. When I mention the *Word* or *Scriptures*, I am referring to both the Old *and* New Testaments.

A difference between the situation in Jesus' day and now is probably this: whereas the Sadducees were ignorant of *both* the Word and the Spirit, I suspect that a vast segment of the church today is often ignorant of one or the other—or the emphasis is on one or the other.

You have those who are knowledgeable of the Word. I call them Word people. You have those who emphasize the Holy Spirit or are knowledgeable of the gifts of the Spirit. I refer to them as Spirit people.

In my experience Word people resent it if someone says they are ignorant of the Holy Spirit. They are indignant. "Whatever do you mean? We believe in the Father, the Son, and the Holy Spirit!" I don't mean to be unfair, but I have sometimes wondered if their true conviction is "God the Father, God the Son, and God the Holy Bible," as Jack Taylor often puts it.

Likewise, Spirit people feel insulted if someone says they are ignorant of the Word—or at least good theology. "We believe in the Bible! That is all we preach!" they will say with fervor. To suggest they don't have much interest in sound theology puts their backs up. They don't get it.

This is why we have the two camps today. Like a divorced couple, they talk past each other, never really listening to each other since each group is totally convinced that they don't have a problem. Hence the problem continues. The church is asleep. The world is going to Hell, and we don't seem to care all that much. We all want to stay in our comfort zones.

There are developments since the 1992 Word and Spirit Conference that I must discuss, although both maladies have been in existence for longer than that.

Charismatic shifts

1. Prosperity teaching

The common denominator that held most Charismatics and Pentecostals together in early years was an emphasis on signs, wonders, miracles, and the gifts of the Spirit—mostly healing. However, that is not true in some Charismatic or Pentecostal ministries today where the emphasis has shifted to prosperity teaching.

Here is partly how it happened. There was an undoubted anointing of healing and miracles in the 1950s. People were truly healed—of cancer, polio (before the Salk vaccine became widely used), and immobility. People in large numbers got out of wheelchairs and either carried their wheelchairs home or threw them away. In the meantime, some of the high-profile people who emphasized healing and who saw people healed began television broadcasts. The money flowed. But for some reason healings started to wane. With fewer genuine miracles, one needed another reason to keep people watching and keep the money flowing.

Around this time, the emphasis switched from healing miracles to financial miracles. Nowadays a TV personality seldom finishes a show without mentioning finances and giving the implication that God does not want you to be poor. I am not saying there is no biblical basis for some of this teaching. I have written a book called *Tithing*, and in it I stress that "you cannot outgive the Lord."[1] However, I fear some have gone too far in their emphasis.

2. Faith healers

Sadly, some who prayed for the sick became known for three things. First, they kept people in wheelchairs away from the front of the auditorium where they would have more hope of receiving prayer. One famous faith healer refused to pray for people in wheelchairs.[2] Second, they began blaming people who needed healing for their lack of faith if they were not healed, giving people with sickness or disability a guilt trip. This sort of thing did not characterize the era of healing anointing that was around decades ago. Third, a spirit of arrogance seems to have emerged in some when it comes to one's own faith. For example, one famous preacher said, "If the apostle Paul had my faith, he would not have had his thorn in the flesh."[3] This kind of teaching is wrong, and many sincere people who don't know solid theology are carried along by it.

Evangelical shifts

1. Avoiding the Spirit

I will not enter much further into the cessationist issue. I have dealt with that in *Holy Fire*. It is my observation, however, that evangelical ministers in general who are not cessationists might as well be. They keep a safe distance from anyone who might cause a stir. They fear losing members or getting involved with anything that might hurt their finances. They remain in their comfort zones. They often seem terrified at any current activity of the Holy Spirit. Moreover, I will repeat what I have said many times: if it were not for the gift of speaking in tongues, there would probably be no objection to the gifts of the Spirit. True revival never comes in a neat and tidy package.

2. Avoiding serious issues

I am disturbed at how rarely anyone opposes Freemasonry. There are Southern Baptists, both pastors and laypeople, in high places who are Masons. Many, many deacons and lay leaders in different denominations in America are Masons, and hardly anyone says a word.

I also must mention the lack of preaching on eternal punishment in most pulpits today. I'm afraid this would include a growing number of Charismatic churches too. Those who have chosen to believe in *annihilationism*—the view that eternal punishment means people come to nothing—have increased dramatically. Also, many of those who reject annihilationism seldom emphasize that the lost will go into conscious eternal punishment after they die.

To summarize, as the church in Ephesus had left their first love, the Gospel, so too have many who believe the Gospel in their heads but do not preach it with passion. Soul winning is never popular.

Furthermore, most people today have never heard of the word *propitiation*—the heart of the Gospel. It means that Jesus' shed blood turned God's wrath away. The justice of God was *satisfied* by the death of His Son. For people to be saved, they need only to transfer their trust from good works to Christ's shed blood.

PERSONAL REFLECTION

Think back to your history in the church. Have you found yourself predominantly on the Word side or the Spirit side? Which has been emphasized more in your spiritual development?

_____

_____

_____

Can you see evidence of some of the maladies discussed above? What are the strengths that you see operating in the Charismatic and Evangelical movements? How could you begin to reconnect those two sides within your own walk with the Lord?

_____

_____

_____

FAULTY EXPERTISE

So awesome are you, O Yahweh, Lord God of Angel Armies!
Where could we find anyone as glorious as you?
Your faithfulness shines all around you!
—PSALM 89:8, TPT

IN MATTHEW 22, when the Sadducees came to Jesus with their biases and prejudices, Jesus said to them, "You are in error because you do not know the Scriptures or the power of God" (v. 29, NIV).

When the crowds heard the way that Jesus expounded the Old Testament, they were "*astonished* at his teaching" (Matt. 22:33, emphasis added). I am fascinated that Jesus' teaching could bring about such an emotion. They were dazzled by His teaching. It is the same Greek word used in Matthew 7:28–29 when, at the end of the Sermon on the Mount, the crowds were "*astonished* at his teaching, for he was teaching them as one who had authority, and not as their scribes." It is the same word used in Luke 9:43 when Jesus cast out a demon; everyone was "astonished."

I often think of the Graham Kendrick song "Restore O Lord." It talks about God restoring the honor of His name. How do you suppose the restoration of that honor is to come about?

Some might say that it will come only through a demonstration of signs, wonders, and miracles. That could be true. However, I believe that God is going to withhold the phenomena of signs and wonders from the church generally until two things coalesce: the Scriptures and the power of God—the Word and the Spirit.

I refer again to where the apostle Paul said, "Our gospel came to you not simply with words but also with power, with the Holy Spirit and deep conviction" (1 Thess. 1:5, NIV). Paul said to the Corinthians: "My message and my preaching were not with wise and persuasive words, but with a demonstration of the Spirit's power" (1 Cor. 2:4, NIV). Paul consistently combined the Scriptures with a demonstration of the power of God—the Word of God and the Spirit of God. Another way of putting it, as we shall examine in more detail later, is that the Word and the name of God will be remarried.

But Jesus' way of putting it in Matthew 22:29 is the combination of the Scriptures and the power of God. The word for *power* is the same as the word used in Luke 24:49 when Jesus said, "Stay in the city until you are clothed with power from on high." It's the word used in Acts 1:8: "You will receive power when the Holy Spirit has come upon you." The two together—the Scriptures and the power of God—are the only explanation for what happened when Peter preached on the day of Pentecost. It was a force that defied a natural explanation. Only God could do it.

To avoid being like the Sadducees in Jesus' day, we ought to know two things they didn't know: the Scriptures *and* the power of God. Both must be emphasized and experienced simultaneously.

The Sadducees mainly descended from priestly families. They traced their ancestry back to the priest Zadok, from whom their name derives. They were the aristocracy of the day, fewer in number than the Pharisees but far more influential in position. The Sadducees didn't *think*—they *knew*; they were the experts on the Law of Moses.

The Sadducees had minimal respect for the prophetic. Their authority was the Pentateuch, the first five books of the Bible. To them, the prophets of the Old Testament were second-class—whether it be the canonical prophets (those who have a book named after them, such as Isaiah or Ezekiel) or the Elijahs or Elishas of Scripture. According to Acts 23:8, the Sadducees' main doctrinal distinctions were (1) no resurrection of the body; (2) no angels; and (3) no such thing as disembodied spirits—they felt that the soul died with the body. They were annihilationists.

The Sadducees despised Jesus of Nazareth. It didn't matter to them that the Pharisees felt the same way about Jesus. They were determined to prove that their doctrinal distinctions were correct and that Jesus was a quickly passing phenomenon.

In the dialogue between Jesus and the Sadducees in Matthew 22:23–32, the Sadducees were very proud of themselves for coming up with an airtight case that would prove their point and put Jesus in His place. "'Teacher,' they said, 'Moses told us that if a man dies without having children, his brother must marry the widow and raise up offspring for him'" (NIV). They followed this legal statement with an illustration. They made it up. It was theoretically possible, but in any case, it suited their purpose. "There were seven brothers among us. The first one married and died, and since he had no children, he left his wife to his brother. The same thing happened to the second and third brother, right on down to the seventh. Finally, the woman died. Now then, at the resurrection, whose wife will she be of the seven, since all of them were married to her?" (NIV).

Jesus was not intimidated by their attempt to ensnare Him. His reply was, "You are in error" (NIV). I once heard William Hendriksen (1900–1982) state it this way: "You are deceived." In a word, "You are ignorant."

Imagine that! Jesus was telling the *experts* in the Pentateuch, "You are *ignorant* of the Scriptures." Could you imagine saying that to a seminary professor, Oxford don, or New Testament scholar?

Then Jesus added, "You're not only ignorant of the Scriptures, but you are also equally ignorant of God's power." Now, why bring that up? They weren't the slightest bit interested in that subject. They had not come to talk about God's power; that was the furthest thing from their minds. It was Jesus who brought it up. Nothing was more irrelevant to them.

I wonder how many Christians today are like that. You have felt that your knowledge of Scripture was enough, that your emphasis upon doctrine was enough. You think that Scripture is all that matters and that talk of God's power was for the apostolic era only.

PERSONAL REFLECTION

Have you experienced the Word in such a way that you were astonished like the crowds listening to Jesus? What were you surprised by, and what did you learn about the nature of God that you hadn't realized before?

_____

_____

_____

Put yourself in the position of the Sadducees, and think back to a time when you were unteachable in some way. What was the cost of that attitude? How did God reveal your error to you?

_____

_____

_____

KNOWING THE WORD

This Book of the Law shall not depart from your mouth, but you shall meditate in it day and night, that you may observe to do according to all that is written in it. For then you will make your way prosperous, and then you will have good success.

—JOSHUA 1:8, NKJV

THE CHURCH TODAY, generally speaking, is like the ancient pharaoh "who did not know Joseph" (Exod. 1:8). Joseph, prime minister of Egypt, had made the children of Israel heroes in Egypt. The fat of the land was theirs. The pharaoh of that time gave them everything they wanted, but that pharaoh died. In the meantime, the children of Israel grew and multiplied. The new pharaoh felt threatened by the growing number of Israelites, and he did not care about Joseph, who had also died. The new pharaoh persecuted the children of Israel. It was as though Joseph never existed.

The church today is filled with millions of pharaohs "who did not know Joseph." There are those who aspire to do God's work but don't know His Word. I heard John Wimber teach at Royal Albert Hall in London that Luther and Calvin gave us the Word in the sixteenth century but that this was the twentieth century, and God wanted us to do the "works."

Later that week I shared my heart with him as lovingly as

I knew how. "John, you are teaching 'pharaohs that knew not Joseph.' You are assuming that the people of the twentieth century have the Word because the Reformers gave us the Word four hundred years ago. Many who are trying to do the works today don't really know the Word."

He laid down his knife and fork, put both forefingers on his chest, and said, "You have touched the very vortex of my thinking right now. I accept what you have said." I felt he meant it, but I never knew if he tried to apply it.

In John 14:26 Jesus said the Holy Spirit would bring to our remembrance what we had been taught. When you read that verse, don't forget that Jesus' disciples had been trained. They were taught by Jesus Himself; they'd heard a lot and learned a lot. Would they forget what they had learned? "Don't worry about that," Jesus said. "The Holy Spirit will bring to your minds what you learned."

I hear people talk about the desire to be Spirit-filled, and I applaud that desire. However, I have to tell you that if you are empty-headed before you are Spirit-filled, you will be empty-headed after you are Spirit-filled. The Spirit cannot remind you of something you never knew in the first place.

I believe that revival is coming—an unprecedented outpouring unlike anything our generation has seen. The question is, Are we ready for it? Have we been trained? Have we been taught? The people God will use most are those who have sought His face (getting to know Him and desiring more *of* Him) rather than His hand (what they can get *from* Him). He is looking for a people who have searched His Word and stood in awe of it.

Job could say, "I have treasured the words of his mouth more than my daily bread" (23:12, NIV). The psalmist could say, "I have hidden your word in my heart that I might not sin against you" (Ps. 119:11, NIV). How many of us memorize Scripture—an art that has virtually perished from the earth? You ask, "What's the use? Why read the Bible? Why memorize Scripture? Why endure teaching? It is so boring; it is so uninspiring."

I answer, "One day it will pay off; the Spirit will bring to your mind what you've learned."

PERSONAL REFLECTION

In what ways have you studied the Scripture? Has biblical teaching felt boring or life-giving to you?

_____

_____

_____

Has the Holy Spirit ever brought a verse or passage of the Bible to mind as a reminder? What effect did that have on your circumstance? If you don't practice this already, choose a verse to memorize this week. Ask the Holy Spirit to bring it to mind whenever you need it.

_____

_____

_____

AN UNPRECEDENTED AWAKENING

The night is almost gone, and the day is near. Therefore let's rid
ourselves of the deeds of darkness and put on the armor of light.
—ROMANS 13:12, NASB

AN UNPRECEDENTED AWAKENING, which I believe is
coming, will come when the Scriptures and the power
of God come together. Another way of putting it is
that the Word and the name of God are rejoined—remarried.
The two ways God unveiled Himself in the Old Testament were
through His Word and His name. "I bow down toward your
holy temple and give thanks to your name for your steadfast
love and your faithfulness, for you have exalted above all things
your name and your word" (Ps. 138:2). The King James Version
got it right, as I keep saying; it reads, "Thou hast magnified thy
word above all thy name."

What is the Word? It came to Abraham, Isaac, and Jacob.
Abraham believed it and was saved. "Abram believed the
LORD, and he credited it to him as righteousness" (Gen. 15:6,
NIV). People are still saved this way, but what does Scripture
say? "'The word is near you, in your mouth and in your heart'
(that is, the word of faith that we proclaim); because, if you
confess with your mouth that Jesus is Lord and believe in your

heart that God raised him from the dead, you will be saved"
(Rom. 10:8–9).

What about the name? It was first disclosed to Moses. It says
in Exodus 3:6—the very verse that Jesus quotes to the Sadducees,
"'I am the God of your father, the God of Abraham, the God of
Isaac, and the God of Jacob.' And Moses hid his face, for he was
afraid to look at God." However, read Exodus 6:2–3: "God also
said to Moses, 'I am the LORD. I appeared to Abraham, to Isaac
and to Jacob as God Almighty, but by my name the LORD I did
not make myself fully known to them'" (NIV).

How could this be? Abraham, Isaac, and Jacob knew and
responded to the Word of God, but they did not know His
name. How is it possible? Because God's Word has priority over
His name. Hearing the Word saves us. That is how God made
Himself known to Abraham. That's how Abraham was saved;
that's how we are saved.

This explains how it is possible for a church to continue
without signs and wonders. Signs and wonders do not save us.
We're saved by the Gospel that tells us Jesus died on the cross
for our sins and rose from the dead. Hearing that Word of grace
and embracing it by faith is what saves us. This is why we will
go to Heaven when we die and not to Hell. The blood that Jesus
shed on the cross two thousand years ago is the most precious
commodity in the history of humanity. The blood that dripped
from His hands, feet, and head cried out to God, and it satisfied
the justice of God. By it we are saved; without it we are lost. It is
hearing that Word that brings us from death to life.

People can see or experience signs and wonders and go to
Hell. People can minister signs and wonders and go to Hell.
Jesus said, "Many will say to me on that day, 'Lord, Lord, did we

not prophesy in your name and in your name drive out demons and in your name perform many miracles?' Then I will tell them plainly, 'I never knew you. Away from me, you evildoers!'" (Matt. 7:22–23, NIV).

I sometimes cannot help but wonder how verses like that make some faith healers and prophetic people feel.

That said, remember that it is also possible to know the Word and be lost. It is possible to be sound in doctrine and never be converted. Some people sit under the ministry of preaching, and you discover to your astonishment that they have never been converted. So don't say that just because you're sound in doctrine, you're going to Heaven. You can be sound in doctrine and be lost. The devil believes and trembles (Jas. 2:19).

PERSONAL REFLECTION

Think back to your own conversion experience. How did the truth of the Gospel reach you in your unbelief? What drew you toward the reality of the cross?

_____

_____

_____

In what way have you experienced signs and wonders from God? What has witnessing His power done to impact your faith and teach you more about His nature?

_____

_____

_____

SIGNS AND WONDERS

So Paul and Barnabas stayed for a long time, speaking
boldly and confidently for the Lord, who continued
to testify to the word of His grace, granting that signs
and wonders (attesting miracles) be done by them.
—ACTS 14:3, AMP

MAKE NO MISTAKE: The Gospel of Jesus Christ is
complete without signs and wonders. However, the
Bible is not complete without signs and wonders.

One day God appeared to Moses. Moses got up that
morning not knowing that day would be different. He was
watching sheep at the foot of Mount Horeb and saw a bush
on fire. Perhaps there was nothing unusual about that; maybe
he'd seen it before. But he noticed something different this
time: the bush didn't burn up. One of two things would be
true. Either the bush was different or the fire was different. He
began to look more closely.

Many want what Moses wanted. He wanted a rational
explanation for what was happening. We all have our questions. Some things are too deep to be revealed this side of
eternity. God said simply, "Stop. Take off your shoes. You are
on holy ground." (See Exodus 3:5.) In that event—an event
through which Moses would never again be the same—God

unveiled His name: "I AM WHO I AM" (Exod. 3:14). He went on to say that He revealed Himself to Abraham, Isaac, and Jacob as God Almighty, but He didn't reveal His name to them.

Unprecedented phenomena—signs and wonders—accompanied the unveiling of God's name. They began with the burning bush. They continued with Aaron's rod, which was turned into a serpent, and with the ten plagues of Egypt, culminating with the night of Passover and the crossing of the Red Sea on dry ground. An unprecedented kind of power inaugurated the revelation of God's name. Signs and wonders defied a natural explanation.

How do we summarize the relationship between His Word and His name? The Word relates to God's integrity: His promise, His grace, His inability to tell a lie. It is the way we are saved. His name refers to His honor: His reputation, His power, and His influence. So while God's Word refers to His integrity, His name refers to His vindication.

However, the Sadducees knew about neither. "You are in error," said Jesus, "because you do not know the Scriptures or the power of God" (Matt. 22:29, NIV). *They didn't even know what Exodus 3:6 really meant*—that the issue behind that verse was the honor of God. Whatever happened to Abraham, Isaac, and Jacob? Were they just relics of the past? Did they die like dogs or cattle or trees?

Jesus gave the Sadducees the shock of their lives. He turned their smug interpretation on its heels and with it affirmed not only the resurrection of the dead but angels and immortality of the soul as well. The existence of an intermediate state demands the resurrection of the body. He said to them in Matthew 22:30, "At the resurrection people will neither marry nor be given in marriage; they will be like the angels in heaven" (NIV). *Resurrection* means the end of death. There will be no need for the procreation of the race. We will be like the angels in Heaven.

At this point Jesus said, as it were, "[Oh, by the way,] about the resurrection of the dead—have you not read what God said to you, 'I am the God of Abraham, the God of Isaac, and the God of Jacob'? He is not the God of the dead but of the living" (vv. 31–32). In other words, Abraham, Isaac, and Jacob are alive and well. They are in Heaven right now with the angels. Their souls and their disembodied spirits are with the Lord at this moment, worshipping Him.

At the natural level, and often in the wrong sense, we all want power. This is why people want a pay raise. This is why people want a promotion. In 1960 John F. Kennedy (1917–1963) was asked, "Why do you want to be president?" He said, "Because that's where the power is."[1]

In a spiritual dimension, we should be greedy for power. Jesus said, "Stay in the city until you are clothed with power from on high" and "You will receive power when the Holy Spirit has come upon you" (Luke 24:49; Acts 1:8). As we have seen, the apostle Paul warned us against "having a form of godliness but denying its power" (2 Tim. 3:5, NIV).

What then is the basis of God giving spiritual power to His followers? I identify four aspects:

1. Personal reading of the Scriptures: We have
   to ask ourselves these questions: "Have I read
   my Bible? Have I read it completely through?"

There are those who have no Bible reading plan, no plans even to have a plan. Jesus would say to you, "You don't know the Scriptures." A strong personal prayer life and reading of the Scriptures daily are the first steps to Holy Spirit power.

2. Personal revelation of the Scriptures: Notice how Jesus put it. "Have you not read what God said to *you*?" (Matt. 22:31, NIV, emphasis added). In other words, Jesus said, "It's for you, Sadducees." However, if it was available to the Sadducees, it is available for anybody. When is the last time that God's Spirit went right through to your heart like a laser beam when you were reading your Bible?

3. Personal rethinking of the Scriptures: You perhaps know the familiar words of Exodus 3:6; they became almost a cliché: "I am . . . the God of Abraham, the God of Isaac, and the God of Jacob." These words were as well known to the Sadducees as a verse like John 3:16—the Bible in a nutshell—is to most of us.

    Many of us lock ourselves in to a point of view concerning certain Bible verses or teaching, just like the Sadducees. Some of us think we know it all. We have accepted a hand-me-down point of view with no questions asked. There is often no personal rethinking by which we acquire the real meaning of any verse. It comes by emptying ourselves before the Lord. Come to Him with openness, saying to Him, "Lord, is it possible I have it wrong when it comes to understanding this verse or this point of view?"

4. Personal release of the Spirit: For many of us this is the hardest thing of all to do. It means giving up any "claim" upon God—a feeling of entitlement, as if He owes us something. This is a major step of faith.

   For some it might seem unbecoming to talk about releasing the Most High, releasing the Holy Spirit, or setting God free, but it is true. We bind the Spirit by holding on to our fear or remaining in our comfort zones. We release the Spirit not only by totally forgiving every single person on earth but also by stepping out in faith to do what He has commanded.

PERSONAL REFLECTION

How often do you read the Bible all the way through? Ideally, what do you want your personal prayer life and Scripture-reading schedule to look like? How could you take the first step in that direction?

_____

_____

_____

The next time you read the Bible or come across a theological point you disagree with, try asking this question of God: "Is it possible I have it wrong in my understanding?" Allow God to speak to you. How is God inviting you out of your comfort zone in this season?

RELEASING THE SPIRIT

The LORD himself goes before you and will be
with you; he will never leave you nor forsake you.
Do not be afraid; do not be discouraged.
—DEUTERONOMY 31:8, NIV

SIMPLY PUT, RELEASING the Spirit is having the courage to do what God tells you to do. You will know in your heart of hearts what He is putting to you. I had to invite Arthur Blessitt to Westminster Chapel. I had to go to the streets of Buckingham Gate and Victoria personally and talk to passersby about Jesus Christ. I knew I would pay a price, but it was worth it. I had to be willing to sing choruses and modern songs in worship—an unprecedented procedure for us in Westminster Chapel. On June 6, 1982, I had to give my first invitation at the end of a sermon to call people forward to confess their faith—a practice never done in Westminster Chapel before.

Incongruous though it may seem, when I set the Holy Spirit free, I too was set free.

However, we also release the Spirit when we pursue both the fruit and gifts of the Spirit with equal earnestness; when we stop quenching the Spirit by our fear, biases, and stubbornness; and when we let God be God. We release the Spirit when we become willing to forgive those who have hurt us in any way (Eph. 4:30–32). Holding a grudge binds the Spirit; total forgiveness sets Him free. It may be surprising how being devoid of bitterness eradicates so many prejudices.

The release of the Spirit comes from the Spirit Himself. It is what He does, and the proof that He has done it is that you even feel free! Where the Spirit of the Lord is, there is freedom and liberty (2 Cor. 3:17).

As I discussed before, the question to ask is, How are you going to get on good terms with the Spirit? If we want power, it's going to have to come from the Spirit. If we are going to get on good terms with the Spirit, then we have to get on good terms with His book—His greatest product. We honor Him when we show that we love His Word—so much so that we want to know the Bible backward and forward.

Do you say that you love the Holy Spirit? He's asking you today, "Do you really?" A release of the Spirit will result in a personal renewal of power that will restore the honor of God's name.

Forgive me if I'm wrong, but I suspect that when it comes to the theme *Word and Spirit*, Evangelicals seem to be more interested in the Word than they are the Holy Spirit. Charismatics seem to be more interested in the Holy Spirit than they are the Word. It is my view that we must love both equally, pursue both equally, and emphasize both equally.

I fear that some have so little confidence in the authority of the Word that it has hardly crossed their minds how the Word of God can astonish. As we saw earlier, Jesus could astonish people with the Word as easily as He could with signs and wonders.

You might say, "Well, if only I could have Jesus teaching me personally all the time, I too would be astonished."

I answer: You have the greatest expositor with you. He is in you: the Holy Spirit. We will release the Spirit to the degree that we (1) stand in awe of His Word, (2) stop quenching the Spirit by unbelief, and (3) stop grieving the Spirit by bitterness and unforgiveness.

The scope for power, therefore, will be found to the degree that we value His own Word. Signs following will be His seal on us. Power that flows from His name will be in proportion to our love for His Word. When we express that love, don't be surprised to see healings, miracles, signs, and wonders take place even during the preaching of the Gospel. There may be no need for people to get into prayer lines. It can happen right where the people are.

My father named me after his favorite preacher, Dr. R. T. Williams (1883–1946), who used to say to young preachers, "Honor the blood and honor the Holy Ghost." By that he meant that the Gospel should emphasize Jesus' blood and that the Holy Spirit should be in control of the services we lead. We must never upstage the Gospel, but we must be open to the Spirit.

I therefore fear that a silent divorce has taken place between the Word and the Spirit, between the Word and the name, between the Scriptures and the power of God.

When these two—the Word and the power of the Spirit—are brought back together, a remarriage will occur. The simultaneous combination will create a spontaneous combustion. The day will come when those who come to see will hear, and those who come to hear will see.

PERSONAL REFLECTION

Has the Holy Spirit ever prompted you to do something that was uncomfortable for you? How did you respond? What was the effect of your obedience or disobedience?

_____

_____

_____

Even if you are not in full-time ministry, we are all called to follow the Holy Spirit's leading. What could it look like, practically, to be even more open to the Spirit throughout your day?

_____

_____

_____

WHERE PROMISES MEET POWER

"My Spirit who is upon you, and My words which I have put
in your mouth shall not depart from your mouth, nor from
the mouth of your offspring, nor from the mouth of your
offspring's offspring," says the LORD, "from now and forever."
—ISAIAH 59:21, NASB

IT FEELS THRILLING to think of a place where promises (the Word) and power (the Spirit) meet, but how does it work? What is the point of the Word and Spirit coming together? What difference does it make?

I believe there are five levels of the Word and Spirit coming together.

1. Believing it: Let's face it. We either accept this or we don't. We believe it is a valid concept or we don't. Some would say that a separation between the Word and Spirit is a false dichotomy; the Word and Spirit never separate. If one takes the view that the Word and Spirit always flow together and there is no such thing as a separation—or divorce—between the Word and Spirit, then what I've written is false and therefore irrelevant.

2. Emphasizing it: There are those who believe what I have written. They think it is a good word, a timely word. Not only that, one should stress from time to time that the notion of bringing the Word and Spirit together is a good idea. We should see it as an ideal match, namely, for the Word and Spirit to come together.

   At this, then, there are those who nod their heads positively. Some might even say, "We need more of this emphasis," but it is always out there as a future thing to anticipate or pray about, like kicking the can down the road. In the meantime, we have other important things to think about, and nothing ever happens. It is perhaps like those who are not cessationists but who have no worries whether the Word and Spirit ever coalesce simultaneously.

3. Trying it: At Westminster Chapel we began healing services by praying for the sick in connection with the Lord's Supper. Then we moved to praying for the sick every Sunday evening following the preaching. Our deacons acted as elders. Those who wanted the anointing of oil called for the elders of the church (Jas. 5:14) by sitting on the front rows of the church. We did this for the last few years I was at Westminster. We saw genuine healings—not a lot, but some. It was absolutely

worth doing, not only for the healings but also because it brought everyone closer to one another.

We were doing our best to give the Holy Spirit an opportunity to work. My part was preaching the Word. Likewise, we were open to the Spirit by offering the anointing of oil. There is more, however. The entire congregation that remained following the preaching would be in an attitude of prayer. Anyone who did not want to pray or be prayed for was asked to go home or go to the back hall for coffee. This meant that all in the main auditorium were inviting the Holy Spirit to manifest in any way He was pleased to do. A great sense of the presence of God became a regular occurrence for my final days at the chapel.

4. Tasting it: To refer to our practice at Westminster, God indeed gave us a taste, but it was only a *taste*—just enough to make one want more. We saw unquestioned healings and at least one deliverance (a man who did not have a full night's sleep for twenty-five years owing to demonic interference was set free). There were others we would hear about later.

The revival I prayed for never came to Westminster Chapel. Following the visit of Arthur Blessitt in 1982, our Pilot Light ministry brought a huge upheaval for a while—the worst trial of my whole life. But on the other hand, there was an anointing that settled on the chapel that stayed throughout my time there—a sweet presence, great unity, peace, joy, and easy preaching. All of it was a taste of the Word and Spirit coalescing.

5. Experiencing the fullness of power: *Fullness of power* means true revival, which we never had at Westminster Chapel, but it is what I pray for daily—that "Isaac" will come. It will be a move of the Holy Spirit that even exceeds the Great Awakening in New England, the Cane Ridge Revival, the Wesleyan Revival in England, and the Welsh Revival. I don't know where it will begin (possibly in London), but it will be a worldwide phenomenon.

As one prophetic person put it, "There is a resurgence of the fear of the Lord coming—and it will fall suddenly, unexpectedly, and unannounced." It will not be an "encore"; it will be unprecedented. He added that "it is a waste of time telling folks to get ready. It will just come."[1]

I hope he is right. I believe he is right. It is what I live for and long for more than anything in the world. Smith Wigglesworth prophesied it just before he died. It will signal the end of the silent divorce between the Word and Spirit.

Personal Reflection

Do you believe that there is power in the Spirit and the Word coming back together for believers? If so, how could you emphasize this in your life?

_____

_____

_____

How could you intentionally make room in your normal routine for the Holy Spirit to move? How could you pursue experiencing the fullness of power?

_____

_____

_____

ENABLED BY THE SPIRIT

> The Spirit of the Lord is upon me, and he has anointed me
> to be hope for the poor, freedom for the brokenhearted, and
> new eyes for the blind, and to preach to prisoners, "You
> are set free!" I have come to share the message of Jubilee,
> for the time of God's great acceptance has begun.
> —LUKE 4:18–19, TPT

WHILE WHAT I'VE written here is in the context of preaching, I believe Christians in any vocation can apply these principles to their lives. All of us are called to share the Gospel with the lost around us. You may never stand behind a pulpit, but you can reach people that your pastor will never reach with the Gospel. My prayer is that God uses this teaching to ignite the personal ministry of any Christian.

Experimental preaching is my term for anointed preaching. No one has improved upon Phillips Brooks' (1835–1893) definition of preaching, which he gave in his historic Yale lectures. He defined preaching as "the bringing of truth through personality."[1] I would define experimental preaching as "releasing the Holy Spirit to be Himself." I regard preaching as an experiment, a test of whether or not the Holy Spirit can get past me.

Following Aristotle, experimental preaching assumes a thesis or major premise, then a minor premise or hypothesis, and then a conclusion. My thesis is this:

Major premise: the Holy Spirit wants to be Himself to the people I address.

Minor premise: I am the instrument of the Holy Spirit.

Conclusion: the Spirit becomes Himself to those I address.

Experimental preaching is what our fathers called unction. Oddly enough, the words *unction* and *anointing* are used very few times in the New Testament, and the meaning does not fit with what is generally referred to as "preaching with unction." Unction, or anointing, comes from the Greek word *chrisma*—not *charisma*, which comes from a different root. *Chrisma* means "anointing."[2] The root word is *chriō*, from which we get the name Christ, meaning anointed one.[3] There are other Greek words (such as *parrēsia*, which means boldness or freedom, or even various forms of *logos*) that often better express what our fathers called "unction"; thus Paul expressed the wish that he would be given "utterance"—*logos*—in Ephesians 6:19.

There is an unusual Greek word used only in the Book of Acts. *Apophthengomai* is translated three different ways, depending on the tense: "utterance" (2:4), "addressed" (2:14), and "speaking" (26:25).[4] Because of this it is almost impossible to give the exact meaning, but one thing is clear: it refers to speaking aloud, possibly with a raised voice.

I would not want to push this point too far, but it is noteworthy to me that the same Greek word, *apophthengomai*, is used for (1) the ability to speak in tongues (Acts 2:4), which is supernatural; (2) Peter's preaching on the day of Pentecost (v. 14), when he received the highest possible level of unction; and (3) Paul addressing King Agrippa (26:25), a very important moment in Paul's ministry. I cannot be sure why Luke chose this word, but it is interesting that he used it to refer to these three extraordinary events. The implication is that what enabled the disciples to speak in tongues is what enabled Peter to preach as he did and Paul to speak to Agrippa as he did. In other words, all three events refer to unusual power.

To put it another way, what the 120 disciples in the Upper Room could do only as the Spirit enabled them on the day of Pentecost—utter words in other languages—is what Peter did as he preached in his *own* language on the day of Pentecost. For Peter to speak powerfully in his own language, he had to have the same power that enabled the 120 to speak miraculously in other languages.

Many of the Greek words mentioned in these lines at first appear very similar. Some are; some aren't. For example, *charisma* and *chrisma* sound alike and look very much alike, but they come from different root words. I would add that the Greek word *chrisma* is a valid word for experimental preaching (1 John 2:20, 27). It comes from *chriō*, which refers to the act of smearing as with an ointment,[5] similar to when the psalmist referred to the "precious oil poured on the head . . . running down on Aaron's beard" (Ps. 133:2, NIV).

Chrisma is not the same thing as charismata, which means "grace-gift." It doesn't even come from the same Greek word. But sadly today it seems that people are more interested in charismata or charisma than in the self-effacing quality inherent in the *chrisma* anointing.

Right now we need this anointing upon our preaching above all else. In my view unction or anointing alone will open new vistas to make truly great preaching a reality. Were this dimension to be recovered by the modern pulpit, it would do more to restore public respect for the church and the Christian faith than anything else I know.

My thesis, then, is that the Holy Spirit wants to be Himself and reach those I address unhindered, ungrieved, unquenched, and undisguised. It lies within my power to hinder or release the Spirit. The question is, Will I block the Spirit or let Him get past me?

Dr. Lloyd-Jones loved to tell the story of an American couple who crossed the Atlantic some two hundred years ago, hoping to hear Whitefield preach at his tabernacle on Tottenham Court Road, London. The couple said they had a very rough crossing. They came into Southampton very tired, but they inquired whether George Whitefield would be in his pulpit on Sunday. Word came that he would be there, so the next day, still tired from their journey, they sat in the tabernacle with great expectation.

They said that when he stood, he too appeared tired. They thought perhaps he'd been very busy and hadn't had time to prepare. At first his sermon seemed very rambling, and they thought, "What have we done, coming all the way here for this?"

But during the sermon, something indescribable happened and the atmosphere became heavenly. Afterward the couple said they would have crossed a thousand seas to be there. They left the tabernacle physically refreshed from the journey.

Reportedly someone once went up to Whitefield and asked for permission to print his sermon. Whitefield replied, "I have no objection, if you will print the lightning, thunder and rainbow with it."[6]

PERSONAL REFLECTION

We are all called to share the Gospel with those around us. Spend some time today asking the Lord to bring to mind specific individuals He has put in your path. How could you share the hope and freedom of the Gospel with them?

_____

_____

_____

Have you ever felt the presence of God on a song, while reading the Bible, or while listening to a sermon, but you couldn't explain it rationally? How was your heart impacted by this encounter? How could you open yourself up even more to being used by the Holy Spirit throughout your daily life?

_____

_____

_____

THE UNOBSTRUCTED SPIRIT

Do not quench [subdue, or be unresponsive to the
working and guidance of] the [Holy] Spirit.
—1 THESSALONIANS 5:19, AMP

I REMIND YOU OF my thesis: the Holy Spirit wants to be Himself to the people I address. "The spirit indeed is willing, but the flesh is weak" (Matt. 26:41), and yet I am the instrument of the Spirit; I stand between God and people either to intercept or to transmit what the Spirit wants to be and to do. If I do not block the Spirit, He will be Himself to my hearers.

The Spirit can be blocked by words of human wisdom. This is one of my greatest temptations, especially when nearly everything I utter publicly is recorded and will sometimes be in print. So the temptation for me is to write a book rather than preach a sermon. This encourages a lopsided emphasis on the correct use of words.

The apostle Paul was one of the greatest intellectuals in the history of the world, one of the greatest rhetoricians of all time. If anybody could speak with the "wisdom of words," it was he. If you don't believe that, read 1 Corinthians 13. However, if Paul made any effort at all, it was in being careful *not to speak* in such a manner that would call attention to the well-turned phrase rather than to the cross. The great Charles Spurgeon used to say, "Labor to be plain."[1]

We block the Spirit if we don't allow the true meaning of the text to flow unhindered. The anointed preacher should be like a transparent windowpane that calls no attention to itself but enables others to see right through it. When we distort the text, we're like cracked windows or, worse, stained-glass windows that are never intended to be seen through.

We can mishandle a text three ways: first, by treating a verse contrary to its context; second, by importing an idea, however valid, that the text did not call for; third, by superimposing our own idea upon the text.

The Spirit wrote the text, and the Spirit knows what it means. My duty is to discover the meaning of the text, not to sound clever or to import an idea or superimpose my opinion onto the text. The text must speak for itself.

I also block the Holy Spirit when I am not myself or when I try to imitate someone else. We tend so often to suppose that another has some quality that we must not have. We see it in another person and pick up his or her mannerisms. We think, "I'm going to be like that, and everyone's going to think I'm like him."

There was a memorable preacher years ago in Texas who was unusually powerful. He had a powerful anointing on him, but when he got going—nobody knew why he did this—his left hand would come up over his ear. He'd just keep on preaching. They made that man professor of preaching at Southwestern Baptist Theological Seminary in Fort Worth, Texas. You could always tell one of his students! When those young men thought they were "ringing the bell," that left hand would go up over the ear!

I told that story at Southwestern Baptist Theological Seminary, hoping to pull the story out of the woodwork. It worked. An old professor came up to me right after the service. He said, "I know exactly who you mean."

I said, "Well, would you please tell me why that left hand would go over his left ear?"

He said, "It's very simple. He was hard of hearing, and he could hear himself better when he spoke like that." But those young men didn't know that. They were simply imitating a weird habit, thinking it was part of the anointing!

Dr. Lloyd-Jones told a similar story. He said, "There was a man in South Wales who had an eccentric habit. When he preached, his hair would get down in his eyes. He wouldn't take his hand and push it back; he would shake it back. Sure enough, young preachers all over South Wales began shaking their heads when they were preaching." Lloyd-Jones added that one of the preachers who began shaking his head was bald!

It is the hardest thing in the world for some of us to come to terms with our own personality. I had to admit a long time ago that I am no Martyn Lloyd-Jones—to accept myself and risk what people will think if I am myself. Why? Because I have come to see that I block the Spirit when I am not myself. God made me the way I am; He made you the way you are—He threw the mold away when He created you.

We need to learn this. We dignify Him when we accept our-selves. When you learn to like yourself, God likes that. He looks down and says, "Well, I'm glad you like yourself—you know, I made you that way." We therefore affirm Him when we accept ourselves as we are.

PERSONAL REFLECTION

Do you ever feel tempted to follow your own wisdom and block something the Holy Spirit is prompting you to do? What fear do you think rises up in you at the thought of giving the Spirit free rein over your life?

_____

_____

_____

Ask the Lord to share with you a few unique qualities that He intentionally wove into your character. Wait on His response. Ask Him what He loves about your personality. Did anything surprise you about what He said?

_____

_____

_____

BLOCKING THE SPIRIT

The Holy Spirit of God has sealed you in Jesus Christ until
you experience your full salvation. So never grieve the Spirit
of God or take for granted his holy influence in your life.
—Ephesians 4:30, TPT

When we avoid difficult scriptures, we block the Holy
Spirit by not following through with the obvious
meaning of the text and its implications. I suspect
that some preachers don't like to preach through a book in the
Bible or through a chapter verse by verse because they're afraid
to face up to a verse that they know will be coming. They may
not know what the verse means, or they may be afraid to discuss what it means, so they jump around the Scriptures instead.
Sometimes it takes courage to pass on the plain meaning of the
text to the hearers. We may think that it will rob us of a chance
to be eloquent, but to do otherwise will rob them of the simple
truth that all our hearers have a right to hear.

All preachers want to master a text, but great preachers are
mastered *by* the text. When the text masters us, we will state
plainly what the text is saying and follow through with the
application that the Holy Spirit dictates—even if that preaching
gets close to the bone and threatens our lifestyles.

This brings me to my next point. Often we will not preach on a subject because we know there is something in our lives that will be obvious, and we dare not preach on it. I am convinced that many preachers will not preach on tithing because *they* are not tithers. Many preachers do not preach on witnessing because *they* don't do it. Therefore, when it comes to certain verses, we don't like to preach that which will expose our hearts. That is why the Spirit doesn't get through us. The Reformers accused Rome of keeping the Bible from the common people, but we do the same thing if we don't pass on the obvious meaning of the text.

I also block the Spirit when I let a personal concern or emotional involvement get in the way of my preaching. This is sometimes called preaching *at* the people, which will never do. There are five options available to the preacher:

Preaching *for* the people. That's performance.

Preaching *at* the people. That's lack of self-control.

Preaching *down* to people. That's arrogance.

Preaching *up* to people. That's fear.

But there is a transaction that takes place between the throne of grace and the pew when we preach *to* the people. That is our calling. Preaching *at* the people blocks the Spirit and leaves the people oppressed; it is always counterproductive. I know because I've done it. The temptation is to set the record straight. It is a melancholy enterprise called self-vindication. It is assuming that the pulpit is my personal platform. James S. Stewart (1896–1990), in his book *Heralds of God*, quoted Bernard Manning: "The pulpit is no more the minister's than the communion table is his."[1]

When I do not allow the ungrieved Spirit to master my

mind in preparation and control my feelings in the act of preaching, though, I block Him. The Holy Spirit is a very sensitive person—in fact the most sensitive person that ever was. We often say of a sensitive person, "You'd better watch what you say around him or her." We see sensitivity as a defect in another person, calling that person hypersensitive. But the Holy Spirit is very like that! It is alarming that we rarely know, at the time, that we are grieving the Spirit. We don't feel a thing. When Samson gave his secret to Delilah, he didn't feel a thing: "He did not know that the LORD had left him" (Judg. 16:20).

Peter said, "Husbands, in the same way be considerate as you live with your wives . . . so that nothing will hinder your prayers" (1 Pet. 3:7, NIV). I know what it's like to quarrel with my wife. I know too what it's like to have my prayers hindered.

Once on a Saturday morning when Louise and I got into an argument, I slammed the door in anger, went to my desk, got out my pen, and said, "Holy Spirit, now help me to write this sermon I've got to preach tomorrow." I just sat there. It was awful. I was too proud to apologize. Our temper often *gets* us into trouble; pride *keeps* us in trouble.

I seethed for seven hours, getting not one thought for my sermon. When I finally apologized and returned to the same desk, the same Bible, and the same blank sheet of paper, ideas began to pour into my mind so quickly that I could not write fast enough. I got all I needed in forty-five minutes. It just goes to show that we can accomplish more in five minutes when the Spirit comes down than we can in five years when we try to work something up in our strength.

I block the Spirit, therefore, when I do not let the Spirit

master my mind in preparation. When I'm angry, when I'm holding a grudge, when I have not totally forgiven the person who has hurt me deeply, then I have grieved the Spirit. Grieving the Spirit results in the inability to think clearly and hear from God. At least this is so with me.

When the Spirit is Himself in me, He is ungrieved and therefore can master my mind. When this is the case, my preparation is a sheer delight; thoughts come—original insights I could never have thought of—because the Holy Spirit wrote the Bible, and He knows what it means.

Finally, I block the Spirit when I do not let Him master my delivery. In other words, I must have the courage to pass on what the ungrieved Spirit gave me in preparation. I must refuse to let any personal concerns come between my congregation and me when I preach. It can also mean I must be willing to depart from my prepared notes and, if necessary, ruin my sermon.

PERSONAL REFLECTION

Are there any portions of Scripture that you have skipped over because they are too difficult to understand? Return to one of those challenging passages of the Bible today, and ask the Holy Spirit to illuminate the Word for you.

_____

_____

_____

Ask the Holy Spirit if there is any anger, bitterness, or unforgiveness blocking His work in your life. Bring any of those feelings to the Lord today and leave them at the cross, exchanging them for His peace, love, and mercy.

_____

_____

_____

HEARING FROM GOD

For prophecy never had its origin in the human
will, but prophets, though human, spoke from God
as they were carried along by the Holy Spirit.
—2 PETER 1:21, NIV

I BECAME AWARE OF "the prophetic," as it is known in some places today, late in my ministry. Until around 1990 I would have regarded anything prophetic to refer to eschatology, the doctrine of last things. I took an interest in biblical prophecy in my teens—partly because my Nazarene pastor in Ashland, Kentucky, spoke a lot from the Book of Revelation.

By the time I went to Trevecca Nazarene University in 1953, I had it all figured out! I even taught the Book of Revelation there when the professor said, "Next week we will treat the Book of Revelation. Is there anyone here who understands it?" My hand shot up like a rocket. "Brother Kendall, would you like to teach it?"

Without hesitation I replied, "Yes." And so I did—with confidence, arrogance, and total absence of humility. I blush to think of the effect it had on the students there. Let us say that it did not endear me to them—or to the professor, who graciously stepped aside to listen to my ignorance.

As I write this book some sixty years later, two things are true. First, I admit to knowing little, if anything, for sure regarding the Book of Revelation. Second, I have become acquainted with several well-known prophetic people. I would add that I am not sure if I understand the prophetic any more than I do the Book of Revelation. It is shrouded in mystery. I say that because I thought I understood it, but I now realize it is a case of history repeating itself. As I knew little about the Book of Revelation but thought I knew a lot, so too I thought I understood the prophetic but realize I know so little.

I can tell you that I have been immersed in the good, the bad, and the ugly of the prophetic. I know enough to affirm that God can speak today in the same way He spoke to Elijah, but I also know enough to realize that the best of people are people at best. I am better off to know what I know, but I must also say that I know enough to make any honest inquirer almost disillusioned.

You might ask, Why deal with this at all? My answer: because it is so relevant.

I do believe that God speaks directly to people today. To maintain the premise that God speaks directly to people is not *violating* Scripture; it is *upholding* it. As Dr. Lloyd-Jones said again and again, not only to me but also to the Westminster group he used to address every month, "God did not give us the Bible to replace the miraculous, the direct witness of the Spirit, or fresh revelation; it was given to correct abuses."

Jesus Christ is the same yesterday, today, and forever (Heb. 13:8). The Holy Spirit is the same yesterday, today, and forever. God the Holy Spirit may speak directly today, but never something that either adds to or contradicts Scripture.

> Let those of us who are mature think this way, and if in anything you think otherwise, God will reveal that also to you.
>
> —PHILIPPIANS 3:15

Am I to believe that Paul's words do not apply to me? Never. It shows that God can talk to me. Why would God give us the New Testament—and words such as we have in Philippians 3:15—if He cannot reveal His clear correction today? The answer is this: God may speak this way today—namely, to sort us out in a manner where we know not only that we are not being deceived but also that He has a way of keeping us on the straight and narrow road!

Speaking personally, I live to hear directly from God. I will take any word from Him I can get—if indeed it is from Him. But I want to know it is from *Him*. I have been given enough prophetic words, from both strangers and friends, to last a lifetime. I have learned not to dismiss them but to be polite. I have learned not to take them too seriously but to put their words on the back burner and wait for their fulfillment.

A woman in Scotland, whom I had not seen before nor have I seen since, rushed toward me with a word of caution. "I keep seeing your heart. It's your heart. Your physical heart. You need to pay attention to your heart and get it checked." I nodded as kindly as I could but did not take her seriously. I remembered her words a few months later when a cardiologist told me that I had aortic stenosis and would need open-heart surgery—immediately.

God might be pleased to send a prophetic word via Scripture, another person's insights, a hymn, or even an audible voice.

Yes, an audible voice; I have experienced this a few times. Not that you could hear it if you were in the same room, but clearly audible to me. However, I live mostly for insight—thoughts and interpretations of God's Word that I've never seen before. I am in my highest realm of ecstasy when this happens.

PERSONAL REFLECTION

What has your experience with prophecy been like? Have you received a prophetic word that you knew was from the Lord, either in the moment or because it was proven true afterward?

_____

_____

_____

How have you experienced God speaking to you? Have you ever heard His audible voice? What impact did that have on your life?

_____

_____

_____

LEVELS OF PROPHECY

Do not despise prophecies. Test all things; hold fast
what is good. Abstain from every form of evil.
—1 THESSALONIANS 5:20–22, NKJV

PROPHECY—IF IT IS true prophecy—is a word directly
from God unfiltered by human embellishment whether
it pertains to the past, present, or future. But not all
prophecy is of the same caliber. There are levels of prophecy as
in a pyramid, starting from the bottom and working to the top.

6. General exhortation (encouragement): Dr.
   Michael Eaton called this "low-level prophecy."
   Paul encouraged this kind of prophecy (1 Cor.
   14:1ff.); he was not motivating someone to
   become another Elijah. Someone may have a
   "word"—whether from a hymn, dream, or even
   a vision—but such a word needs to be tested.
   As I have said, we are not to despise such
   prophesying (1 Thess. 5:19–20), but all words
   need testing.

5. Specific warnings: Certain disciples urged Paul
   not to go on to Jerusalem. Luke sides with

143

them; he says that they warned Paul "through the Spirit" (Acts 21:4). Agabus similarly warned Paul, saying, "The Holy Spirit says" (v. 11, NIV), and yet Paul refused to heed their warnings. Who got it right? Was Paul wrong to ignore them? Agabus may have been wrong; Paul may have been wrong. In any case, it did not seem to bother Paul; he went to Jerusalem anyhow.

4. Prophetic preaching: Peter said one should speak as if his or her words were the "very words of God" (1 Pet. 4:11, NIV). I wish this were the case in my own preaching. My basic style is expository and pastoral, but nothing thrills me more than when someone says to me, "How did you know I was there today? That is exactly what I needed." Expository preaching can be prophetic without the preacher being conscious of this. Even if the preacher is conscious of the Lord's enabling, he or she should be humble about it and not say, "Thus says the Lord."

3. When forced to testify during persecution: Jesus said, "When they arrest you, do not worry about what to say or how to say it. At that time you will be given what to say, for it will not be you speaking, but the Spirit of your Father speaking through you" (Matt. 10:19–20, NIV). In the autumn of 1963, when I was pastor of a small church in Carlisle, Ohio, I was called before a group of ministers to answer charges that came

from some of my church members. On the
morning of my heresy trial, I supernaturally
received Matthew 10:19–20 from the Lord. I
felt His help that evening when answering a
"heretical" charge that I claimed Jesus is God.
I pleaded guilty to that charge! Those present
assured me that I won the day. God gave me the
exact words to say. It was the first time I needed
to lean on Jesus' promise in Matthew 10:19–20.

2. Noncanonical prophecy: Nathan, Gad, Elijah,
    and Elisha are examples of noncanonical
    prophets. Could there be prophets of this
    magnitude and stature today? I believe so. Then
    can they say, "The Lord told me"? I reply: they
    should be the wariest of all in saying things
    such as "the Lord says." Why? They will be
    watched and examined with the most painful
    scrutiny. If they will keep the name of the
    Lord out of it and simply say something like "I
    feel I must say this to you," they will maintain
    their integrity, credibility, and anointing.
    Many modern prophets could have been saved
    incalculable embarrassment had they been more
    modest in their claims. You lose *nothing* by
    keeping the name of the Lord out of the picture.
    You embarrass the angels when you include
    the name of the Lord and get it wrong. There
    is no need to bring in the name of the Lord

when passing a caution or encouragement to someone.

1. Holy Scripture: This includes all of the Old Testament, with the canonical prophets, and all of the New Testament. Scripture is God's final revelation. No one will ever have the authority to speak like this. If any man or woman claims to speak on the same level as Holy Scripture, he or she is utterly out of order and will be found out sooner or later. Only the Bible is infallible.

PERSONAL REFLECTION

Which levels of prophecy have you experienced or seen in action? Have you ever given an encouraging prophetic word to someone else? How did hearing it impact that individual?

_____

_____

_____

Have certain passages of Scripture, previously highlighted by the Holy Spirit, served as prophetic revelation for your life? What were those passages? What guidance or encouragement did they bring?

_____

_____

_____

LIMITS TO PROPHECY

You shall not take the name of the LORD your God in
vain [that is, irreverently, in false affirmations or in ways
that impugn the character of God]; for the LORD will not
hold guiltless nor leave unpunished the one who takes His
name in vain [disregarding its reverence and its power].
—EXODUS 20:7, AMP

THERE ARE LIMITS to prophecy. First, remember that
each of us has but a "measure of faith" (Rom. 12:3). This
means there is a limit to our faith. Only Jesus had a perfect faith because He alone had the Holy Spirit without limit
(John 3:34).

Second, for those who prophesy, it must be done in two ways:
(1) in "proportion" to their faith (Rom. 12:6), not going beyond
the anointing; and (2) according to the analogy of faith. The
Greek word translated "proportion" is *analogia*.[1] This means
comparing scripture with scripture, making sure you are within
the bounds of sound theology!

Third, remember that prophecies will cease (1 Cor. 13:8–9).
This means there are seasons of the prophetic. The word of the
Lord was "rare" at one time in ancient Israel (1 Sam. 3:1). Amos
spoke of a famine of hearing the word of the Lord (Amos 8:11).

This means that sometimes God chooses to say nothing. God

may choose not to speak for a generation. If so, how foolish to pretend to speak for Him. Rare is that prophetic person who will refuse to be drawn out to give a "word" when there is not clearly such a word! A common mistake of many prophetic people is that they have some form of "spiritual experience" and get a genuine word from God but then embellish it with personal exhortation or theological teaching based on their own experience to justify the spin, which may or may not be from God.

Fourth, Paul said that "we know in part and we prophesy in part" (1 Cor. 13:9). This means nobody knows everything and no prophet has unlimited knowledge. That should keep all those with an undoubted prophetic gift humble!

There are certain principles we must follow to maintain transparent integrity regarding the prophetic. First, don't go beyond what you are given. This is much the same thing as Paul instructing the Corinthians "not to go beyond what is written" (1 Cor. 4:6). So too with a prophetic word; do not embellish it. I have known more than a few prophetic people who receive an undoubted word from the Lord but end up messing it up by embellishing it.

Second, be very, very careful to honor the name of the Lord. Here is what is stated in James 5:12: "But above all, my brothers, do not swear, either by heaven or by earth or by any other oath, but let your 'yes' be yes and 'no' be no, so that you may not fall under condemnation." This warning is addressed to poor Christians who had been mistreated by well-to-do Christians, as pointed out in verses 1–6. The temptation for both was to claim "God is on our side" by bringing in God's name. James' word: do not do that. Do not abuse that name by claiming God is with you and not them. In other words, says James, leave God's name out of it. Quit using His name to make yourselves look good.

This is why a prophetic person should be careful not to say, "Thus says the Lord" or "The Lord told me." Why? Because you are claiming to have inside knowledge that God has spoken through you—using God's name to make yourself look good. When we do that, we are not trying to make *God* look good; we are trying to make ourselves look good. This breaks the third commandment that says we must not misuse the name of the Lord (Exod. 20:7). It is taking God's name in vain when you *use* His name to puff up your prophetic utterance.

Misusing God's name is when you bring Him into your conversation to elevate your own credibility. You are thinking of yourself, not Him. Perhaps you want people to think you are spiritual. You want to seem close to God.

I have done this too often over the years—I am ashamed to say. I have (I hope) stopped it. I believe I am to share this with everybody in these last days. Did the *Lord* tell me to share this? You tell me!

The issue here is the oath. One of the greatest privileges Christians can have is for God to swear an oath to you and me the same way He did to Abraham. The oath is seen when God grants the highest level of faith; this is what lay behind the miraculous in the Bible. If granted, the oath from God to us may pertain to (1) assurance of salvation (Heb. 4:10; 10:22); (2) advanced notice of answered prayer (Mark 11:24; 1 John 5:15); (3) knowing you have it right theologically (Col. 2:2); (4) the prayer of faith for healing (Jas. 5:15); and (5) a prophetic word (1 Pet. 4:11).

All prophecy must be done in proportion to our faith; it is only when the oath is given to us that we know for certain we have been given a word from God. This is what lay behind Elijah's authority. As I show in *These Are the Days of Elijah* (Chosen Books), Elijah had authority before Ahab because of God's oath to him. Only when God swears an oath to you can you have the kind of authority that Elijah had before Ahab. Elijah did not bite his nails for several years wondering if he saw a cloud in the sky. He calmly said to the king, "It won't rain unless I say so." How could Elijah be so sure? "As the LORD, the God of Israel, lives, before whom I stand, there shall be neither dew nor rain these years, except by my word" (1 Kings 17:1). That is oath language.

Any prophecy should make *God* look good, not the prophet. If you disagree with what I have said and decide to say, "Thus says the Lord," you had better know *absolutely* what you are claiming—namely, that God has sworn an oath to you.

I am not saying, then, that you should never say, "The Lord told me" or "Thus says the Lord." I am urging you never to say it unless you have that oath-level assurance that God has spoken. Even then, you don't *have* to say it!

If you leave the Lord's name out, you won't regret it. You can always say, "I am compelled to share this with you" if you believe the Lord has spoken. You are also safe if the word is not from above. You will not be embarrassed, and you will not have abused God's name.

Remember, James said, "Above all" do not misuse the Lord's name "so that you may not fall under condemnation" (Jas. 5:12). Misusing His name isn't worth it.

PERSONAL REFLECTION

How do you feel about people concluding their prophetic words with "Thus says the Lord"? Have you used the Lord's name in this way? What do you think was your motivation, if so?

_____

_____

_____

Imagine the confidence that Elijah had in the word of God in order to tell Ahab it wouldn't rain. Has God ever sworn an oath to you? What makes you feel confident in hearing God's voice?

_____

_____

_____

ISAAC IS COMING

Trust in the Lord completely,
and do not rely on your own opinions.
With all your heart rely on him to guide you,
and he will lead you in every decision you make.
Become intimate with him in whatever you do,
and he will lead you wherever you go.
—PROVERBS 3:5–6, TPT

Jonathan Edwards taught us that the task of every generation is to discover which direction the sovereign Redeemer is moving in and move in that direction. One should also remember that Edwards—no doubt the leading light in America's Great Awakening of the eighteenth century—also thought that he was witnessing the prophecy of Habakkuk in his own day. It is sometimes called "the latter-day glory"—an era that will precede the second coming of Jesus. I join many people in church history who have believed that a major move of the Holy Spirit will encircle the globe before the end. Some of these understandably thought they were seeing this glory in their day. Like them, I believe we will witness it in our day. Time will tell if this essential teaching is from the Lord.

I call this latter-day glory "Isaac." Abraham hoped the

promised son would be Ishmael, but he had to adjust. Many Charismatics have thought the Pentecostal-Charismatic movement of the twentieth century was "it"—the final move of the Holy Spirit before the second coming of Jesus. I believe the best is yet to be: Isaac is coming.

Rolfe Barnard (1904–1969), one of my early Calvinist mentors, played a significant role in my grasp of Charismatics. Whereas many of Rolfe's fellow ministers and followers largely dismissed the Pentecostals and Charismatics from consideration as movements of God, Rolfe definitely had a different perspective. He believed God was in these movements. He was especially intrigued by David du Plessis (1905–1987), the South African Pentecostal.

However, Rolfe's verbatim comment regarding the Charismatic movement was "I believe that God is in it, but that's not *it*." That was his way of saying there would be something much greater to come—namely, the latter-day glory.

In the autumn of 1973, a few weeks after I arrived in Oxford, I went to hear du Plessis at a special meeting there. I had learned that Smith Wigglesworth made a significant prophecy to du Plessis, and because Rolfe spoke favorably of him, I didn't want to miss it. I'm glad I went, but to be candid, I found him more than a little disappointing. I expected more. Little he said rang true with me. I certainly agreed with Rolfe: "This is not *it*." Over the next several months I was gripped by the notion that the Charismatic movement could be compared to Ishmael and that Isaac represents the genuine latter-day glory.

Did I get this from the Lord? You tell me. I shared this

first at my church in Lower Heyford, Oxfordshire. The members of Westminster Chapel will remember this comparison very well. I shared it with Dr. Lloyd-Jones. He did not commit to it but clearly liked the idea. If you put me under a lie detector, I would say it was from the Lord, but at the end of the day, we will have to wait and see what happens.

Never in my life had I known fear and trembling as I felt in the days before I originally gave this message at the Wembley Conference Centre in October 1992. My writing in this book is an elaboration of what I proposed on that evening.

I was forecasting a new era, one that can be called a post-Charismatic era.

When I use the term *Charismatic*, I see it as shorthand for the work of the Spirit—including with Pentecostals—that we've all known about throughout the past century.

A few days before the Word and Spirit Conference, Lyndon Bowring and I had a meal with a respected Charismatic leader. Quite spontaneously I put this question to him: "If the Charismatic movement is either Ishmael or Isaac, which do you think it is?"

He answered, "Isaac."

I said to him, "What if I told you that the Charismatic movement is not Isaac but Ishmael?"

His answer was "I hope not."

This man, a Spirit-filled, godly man, responded exactly as Abraham did: "And Abraham said to God, 'If only Ishmael might live under your blessing!'" (Gen. 17:18, NIV).

God was handing Abraham what he had wanted more than anything in the world—the promise of a son through his beloved wife, Sarah—and he was rejecting it! When God's promise was originally given, I'm sure Abraham would never have believed that one day he would react so negatively to something so positive.

That is largely the way many Charismatics reacted to my address that evening. The point that Isaac is coming—something more significant than we have ever seen—did not compensate for the pain they felt that night. "You call us Ishmael," a close Charismatic friend said to me. "But Isaac is coming," I stressed.

It was hard for some Charismatics to accept the notion that the movement they gave their lives for and endured persecution for was not "it" after all. I understood that. However, the same Charismatic friend I just quoted has since embraced my position. Indeed, now that it is almost thirty years later, Charismatics almost everywhere are saying to me, "We hope you are right. Because if what we now have is all there is, the future is pretty bleak."

PERSONAL REFLECTION

Has God ever asked you to lay something that you loved down so that you might receive something greater from Him? What was that process like for you? What would have happened if you had relied on your own opinions instead?

_____

_____

_____

Where do you see God moving within the church and outside it today? Are there any aspects of what you see Him doing that make you uncomfortable or nervous? Spend some time recommitting yourself to complete trust in Him alone.

_____

_____

_____

DAY 36

GRIEVING ISHMAEL

Behold, I will do a new thing; now it shall spring
forth; shall ye not know it? I will even make a way
in the wilderness, and rivers in the desert.
—ISAIAH 43:19, KJV

FOR THIRTEEN YEARS Abraham sincerely believed that Ishmael was the promised son. It all began years earlier when he was given a promise from God. Indeed, believing that promise meant that righteousness was put to his credit.

Abraham might have said to God, "Do You expect me to believe that? You must be joking. I am eighty-five, and Sarah is seventy." But no, Abraham believed it. By believing the promise, righteousness was credited to Abraham. This became the apostle Paul's chief illustration for the doctrine of justification by faith (Rom. 4). It was what Martin Luther rediscovered in the sixteenth century, and it turned the world upside down.

Here is the Gospel in a nutshell: when we believe that Jesus died on the cross for our sins, and we transfer all the hope we once placed in our works onto what Jesus did for us on the cross, righteousness is put to our credit as though we had never sinned. That is the Gospel.

Abraham believed that promise, but the years were rolling by. No son. Sarah was getting older. No son. She was far past the age in which it was usually possible for a woman to bear a child. Abraham and Sarah were both discouraged. We all get discouraged when God delays the fulfillment of His word. We all tend to fret during the era of unanswered prayer. We all know the pain of waiting, having been sure that we got it right. Abraham had been sure when God said that He would make Abraham's descendants as numerous as the stars in the sky (Gen. 15:5), but nothing was happening.

One day Sarah came up with a solution:

> Now Sarai, Abram's wife, had borne him no children. But she had an Egyptian slave named Hagar; so she said to Abram, "The LORD has kept me from having children. Go, sleep with my slave; perhaps I can build a family through her."
>
> Abram agreed to what Sarai said. So after Abram had been living in Canaan ten years, Sarai his wife took her Egyptian slave Hagar and gave her to her husband to be his wife. He slept with Hagar, and she conceived.
>
> —GENESIS 16:1–4, NIV

Abraham did not initiate this idea; it was entirely Sarah's. Why did he agree to it? Because Abraham really did believe the promise, and he was willing to see it happen any way God chose to bring it about. What is more, if Hagar's child happened to be a male, having come from Abraham's own body, it would fulfill the promise. That would give every reason to believe that God was at work. A male child would fit the promise of Genesis 15:4–5.

Ishmael was born when Abraham was eighty-six. As far as Abraham was concerned, God had kept His word. There could be no doubt about it. Everything pointed to Ishmael's being the promised son, and so Abraham said to God, "If only Ishmael might live under your blessing" (Gen. 17:18, NIV).

Abraham had not only become reconciled to the suggestion that Hagar should be the mother of his son, but he also saw that it seemingly met every condition of the promise of Genesis 15:4—every condition he ever imagined. Genesis 15:4, as far as Abraham was concerned, was now ancient history; *it was done.* God had kept His word; that was that. Ishmael met the requirements, and Abraham had no complaints.

One day Abraham got up like on any other morning, unprepared for what would happen on that day. What a difference a day makes! Abraham was now ninety-nine years old, and Ishmael, his pride and joy, was a teenager. Never underestimate how much Abraham loved Ishmael, his one and only son. Then out of the blue, God appeared to Abraham.

God gave him the covenant of circumcision, the incredible promise that he would be the father of many nations; the land of Canaan would be an everlasting possession; he loved every moment of it. Everything was going fine with Abraham.

Moreover, no problem about the circumcision—Abraham would circumcise Ishmael and would himself be circumcised. The covenant would extend to his household, even to foreigners who became a part of his household. The covenant was inflexible; not to keep it was to forfeit the promise. That was fine. So far, so good.

Then came some news for which Abraham was unprepared. It ought to have been the grandest, sublimest, most fantastic promise that his ears would ever hear. However, he couldn't believe what he was hearing, and he didn't like it.

> And God said to Abraham, "As for Sarai your wife, you shall not call her name Sarai, but Sarah shall be her name. I will bless her, and moreover, I will give you a son by her. I will bless her, and she shall become nations; kings of peoples shall come from her." Then Abraham fell on his face and laughed and said to himself, "Shall a child be born to a man who is a hundred years old? Shall Sarah, who is ninety years old, bear a child?" And Abraham said to God, "Oh that Ishmael might live before you!"
> —GENESIS 17:15–18

Abraham's world was now turned upside down. He was uttering an impassioned, painful plea, "Please let the covenant be fulfilled in Ishmael."

I am prepared to say that this is precisely what God is saying to us at the present time. Sarah, whom the apostle Paul called "the mother of us all" (Gal. 4:26, NKJV), will conceive. For all I know, she has already conceived. Someone said that Isaac will be an "ugly baby" but a handsome man when he comes of age. The hidden, sovereign work of the Holy Spirit often emerges in the least likely people and places. However much we love Ishmael—the Pentecostal and Charismatic movements—however much God affirmed Ishmael, and however much Ishmael fit what many hoped for, God is up to something new. God was behind Ishmael, but Ishmael is not God's ultimate purpose. Sarah will conceive. Isaac will show up any day.

PERSONAL REFLECTION

Think back to a time when you received a promise from the Lord. Was there ever a temptation to fulfill that promise by your own hand? How does self-sufficiency impact your ability to trust in God's timing and guidance?

_____

_____

_____

Does your spirit resonate with the prophecy that God is up to something new? Spend some time with the Lord, asking Him to reveal His heart to you for this new Isaac season.

_____

_____

_____

GOD HEARS

For the eyes of the Lord are toward the righteous,
and His ears attend to their prayer.
—1 PETER 3:12, NASB

TODAY WHEN WE consider how God has blessed the church through the Charismatic and Pentecostal movements and how many wonderful and thrilling things have come during this era, what will Isaac be like?

Abraham did not initiate the era of Ishmael. He was an honorable man who believed God's promise. Sarah, the mother of us all, was the instigator of the whole thing, and we should honor her. The promise of a son came to Abraham as a word from God. Furthermore, God's affirmation of Ishmael to Hagar proves it was of God.

The Charismatic era is of God. He did it, and we're all the better for it. Most churches worth their salt today in the United Kingdom—England, Wales, Scotland, and Northern Ireland—are Charismatic. Whereas in the United Kingdom the Charismatic movement is mainstream, such is seen in the United States as the lunatic fringe. This is all the more reason there is a stigma in the United States against upholding all the gifts of the Spirit.

The greatest hymnody that the last one hundred years have seen has emerged from the Charismatic movement. From Graham Kendrick to Matt Redman to Hillsong, where would we be today without their contributions? When you consider that the widespread revival, particularly in Africa, Latin America, South America, Indonesia, and Korea, is largely Pentecostal, you can see why we should affirm the Charismatic era.

Sarah persecuted Hagar. Consider how much Charismatics and Pentecostals have suffered, mainly from Evangelicals! Pentecostals, neo-Pentecostals, those who dare talk about the gifts of the Spirit, signs, wonders, and miracles, have been "outside the camp"—like Hagar in the desert. They have been put down, lied about, misunderstood, and persecuted as much as those in any era in the history of the Christian church.

An undoubted divine visitation affirmed Hagar in the desert. She could look up to God through her tears. I love the way the King James Version puts it; it moves me almost to tears every time I read it: Hagar "called the name of the Lord that spake unto her, Thou God seest me" (Gen. 16:13). Hagar knew that God had given her a son. God even gave the son the name Ishmael, which means "God hears." God left Hagar in no doubt that He was with her, that He was behind it all. Likewise, those who unashamedly regard themselves as Charismatics know that God has visited them; God has affirmed them. They have seen the supernatural. My heart warms to them; they are among my closest friends; I am one of them.

It is not all worked up. Undoubted signs and wonders have characterized Pentecostals and Charismatics all over the world. It is sad that much of the Charismatic movement has allowed prosperity teaching to replace the supernatural.

Furthermore, God had a secret purpose for Ishmael that was revealed first to Hagar and later to Abraham.

> The angel of the Lord also said to [Hagar], "I will surely multiply your offspring so that they cannot be numbered for multitude."
>
> —Genesis 16:10

> As for Ishmael, I have heard you; behold, I have blessed him and will make him fruitful and multiply him greatly. He shall father twelve princes, and I will make him into a great nation. But I will establish my covenant with Isaac.
>
> —Genesis 17:20–21

We haven't seen the end of this yet, by the way. The natural, literal, Arabic descendants of Ishmael are too numerous to count. They have spread in ever-increasing numbers, and their mosques and places of worship are going up rapidly in every major city. Who knows what the end will be? We are going to see Muslims turning to Christ before it is all over. "'What no eye has seen, nor ear heard, nor the heart of man imagined, what God has prepared for those who love him'— these things God has revealed to us through the Spirit" (1 Cor. 2:9–10).

PERSONAL REFLECTION

How have you benefited from the Charismatic movement? Have any of the teachings or worship songs impacted your walk with God for the better?

_____

_____

_____

Think back to a time when, like Hagar, you felt abandoned by those around you. How did God show that He saw and heard you during that season?

_____

_____

_____

THE PROMISED CHILD

For all of God's promises find their "yes" of
fulfillment in him. And as his "yes" and our
"amen" ascend to God, we bring him glory!
—2 CORINTHIANS 1:20, TPT

ISHMAEL WAS NOT meant to be the promised child. God
wanted the promise of the Gospel as revealed to Abraham
to be fulfilled in a manner that defied a natural explanation. Conversion is the greatest miracle that can happen under
the sun. It is a sovereign work of God; it is what God does.
When Hagar conceived, it was natural, but when Sarah conceived, it defied a natural explanation; only God could have
done it.

God wanted the heirs of the Gospel to look back on what
He did in a manner no one would question. Understandable
though it was for Abraham to agree with Sarah's proposal,
there would always be a cloud over it.

Isaac will appear suddenly when the church generally is in
a deep sleep, expecting nothing. There are at least two occur-
rences in Scripture that point to the same thing: the prophecy
of Malachi and the parable of the ten virgins.

Malachi 3:1–4 says:

I send my messenger, and he will prepare the way before me. And the Lord whom you seek will suddenly come to his temple; and the messenger of the covenant in whom you delight, behold, he is coming, says the LORD of hosts. But who can endure the day of his coming, and who can stand when he appears? For he is like a refiner's fire and like fullers' soap. He will sit as a refiner and purifier of silver, and he will purify the sons of Levi and refine them like gold and silver, and they will bring offerings in righteousness to the LORD. Then the offering of Judah and Jerusalem will be pleasing to the LORD as in the days of old and as in former years.

Although John the Baptist himself fulfilled Malachi's prophecy, the latter part of Malachi's word says that the Jews and Jerusalem will be pleasing to the Lord "as in the days of old and as in former years." That was not the case when Jesus came on the scene. They rejected Him. The references to Levi and Judah and Jerusalem are therefore unfulfilled. Instead of the Jews in Jerusalem pleasing the Lord, the opposite was true. Jesus wept over Jerusalem because they forfeited what belonged to them, owing to their rejection of their promised Messiah.

In other words, Malachi's prophecy that the Jews and Jerusalem would please the Lord must still be future! However, I will add this: Isaac will be a John the Baptist–type ministry. As John the Baptist prepared the way for Jesus, Isaac—when the Word and the Spirit reunite—will get the bride of Christ ready for the second coming of Jesus.

In the parable of the ten virgins, the bridegroom arrived in the middle of the night. (See Matthew 25:6–10.) Picture yourself at 2:00 a.m. The last thing you want is to be awakened at that hour. Jesus said that in the very last days the church will be aptly described as asleep. When the church generally is decadent, powerless, asleep, and expecting nothing, Isaac will appear.

There will be three categories of Christians at that time: (1) the wise sleeping virgins, (2) the foolish sleeping virgins, and (3) those who actually wake up the church to say, "Here is the Bridegroom! Come out to meet Him." This third category will be comprised of a remnant *not asleep* but available to God the Holy Spirit to wake up the church in the last days.

As one prophetic person put it a few years ago, "There is a resurgence of the fear of the Lord coming—and it will fall suddenly, unexpectedly, and unannounced. A new day is coming! It is not an encore—this will be like no other. This will be a hallmark of a huge wave of the Spirit that will sweep around the earth. It will be about holiness and purity of heart—and it is a waste of time telling folks to get ready. It will just come—Suddenly. A revival with a hallmark of tears, but also profound intimacy, with the person of the Holy Spirit."[1]

One might overlook what the promise of Isaac eventually did for Abraham: it drove him back to God's word. In Romans chapter 4, the apostle Paul, having dealt with Genesis 15:6, shows the basis of his doctrine of justification by faith; he suddenly jumps to the time when Abraham was reconciled to the fact that Isaac was on the way.

> Against all hope, Abraham in hope believed and so
> became the father of many nations, just as it had been

said to him, "So shall your offspring be." Without weakening in his faith, he faced the fact that his body was as good as dead—since he was about a hundred years old—and that Sarah's womb was also dead. Yet he did not waver through unbelief regarding the promise of God, but was strengthened in his faith and gave glory to God, being fully persuaded that God had power to do what he had promised. This is why "it was credited to him as righteousness."

—ROMANS 4:18–22, NIV

It was credited to Abraham as righteousness when he believed the first time. But now he was believing again, and he went back to God's original promise. Abraham now had something to live for that exceeded his greatest expectation. For over the years, Abraham had underestimated the word—the dignity of it, the glory of it. But with the promise of Isaac on the way, once he became reconciled to what God said was going to happen next, it drove him back to the word.

The coming of Isaac will get the church back to the Word of God as we have not done for years. There will be a new romance with the Scriptures. It will be like falling in love all over again. It will result in a fresh assurance, a burst of power, and an expectancy that we never dreamed possible. We will have something to live for, unlike anything we have ever known.

PERSONAL REFLECTION

Has God ever surprised you with how He has answered your prayers? How was the fulfillment of His promise different than your expectation?

_____

_____

_____

How would a sudden resurgence of the fear of the Lord impact your life personally? Spend some time with God, dreaming with Him about what a wave of the Spirit would look like.

_____

_____

_____

THE ERA OF ISAAC

Therefore, since we are receiving a kingdom which cannot be
shaken, let us have grace, by which we may serve God acceptably
with reverence and godly fear. For our God is a consuming fire.
—HEBREWS 12:28–29, NKJV

THE COMING OF Isaac will be characterized by an awe of
God and His Word not seen in our generation. "Who
can endure the day of his coming, and who can stand
when he appears?" (Mal. 3:2). A renewal of the fear of God will
mean a return to holiness. Whatever happened to holiness? "He
is like a refiner's fire and like fullers' soap" (Mal. 3:2). When the
Word and the Spirit coalesce, it will be a remarriage of what
should never have separated. As with human marriage, God
said, "What therefore God has joined together, let not man separate" (Matt. 19:6).

What then will Isaac look like? It will be an era in which the
Word preached will be as awesome as the vindication of God's
name—which means authentic signs, wonders, and miracles. It
will be an era in which signs and wonders will not be under
a cloud of suspicion but open to the minutest scrutiny. As the
New Testament skeptics said of the miracle of the disabled man
who suddenly was walking, "We cannot deny it" (Acts 4:16).

Millions of Muslims will be converted. Thousands of Muslims who have had dreams about Jesus will come out of hiding. This will include imams who are at the moment afraid to discuss this. This phenomenon will dazzle the world.

At the moment, it is virtually impossible to get very far in presenting the Gospel to a Jew. In Israel it is forbidden for a Christian to evangelize. But something—I am not sure what—will cause the light to turn on in the hearts of Jews from all parts of the world. They will be a part of an evangelism effort that leads Jews, Muslims, and people of all races and nations to Christ.

It will be an era when the Gospel, as well as signs and wonders, will be at the forefront of priorities among God's ministers. It will be an era when conversion to Christ will not be minimized but will be seen as the greatest miracle that can happen. It will be an era in which the most difficult cases imaginable will turn into putty in the hands of a sovereign God, when surprising conversions become common. Some of those who have opposed the Gospel the most, laughed at biblical infallibility, and dismissed the historic Christian faith will fall on their faces before God in repentance. It will be an era when the world will fear the prayers of God's people more than they fear nuclear war. Mary, Queen of Scots, is said to have feared John Knox's prayers "more than all the assembled armies of Europe."[1]

The post-Charismatic era will be a time when government and people in high places will come on bended knee to God's people and ask for help. With Ishmael it was the promise of a nation; with Isaac it was the promise of many nations.

The apostle Paul said that Isaac is the "heir of the world" (Rom. 4:13). We're talking about something big. We're talking about something that is wider than one nation's boundaries, when kings of the earth, leaders of nations, are made to see that there is a God in the heavens. It will be an era in which children will be sovereign vessels, an age when ordinary Christians are equipped with prophetic gifts. It won't be a case of religious superstars vying for TV time, trying to be seen or heard or trying to prove themselves. We're talking about an awakening that reaches forgotten areas, cuts into people's hearts, and turns upside down places that heretofore were thought to be impenetrable. All this will come without the aid of the media, public relations firms, or the endorsement of high-profile celebrities.

The coming of Isaac will begin an era in which the glory of the Lord covers the earth as the waters cover the sea.

PERSONAL REFLECTION

How has God been refining you in this season? What aspects of Himself has He been revealing to you?

_____

_____

_____

Consider some of the ways that God is moving in countries that are historically closed to the Gospel. What do those testimonies reveal about the heart of God?

_____

_____

_____

THE AWAKENING OF THE CHURCH

Awake, O my soul, with the music of his splendor-song!
Arise, my soul, and sing his praises!
My worship will awaken the dawn,
greeting the daybreak with my songs of praise!
—PSALM 57:8, TPT

SMITH WIGGLESWORTH IS alleged to have made a prophecy three months before he died that forecast a coming together of the Word and Spirit. This is what he reportedly said:

> During the next few decades there will be two distinct moves of the Holy Spirit across the church in Great Britain. The first move will affect every church that is open to receive it and will be characterized by a restoration of the baptism and gifts of the Holy Spirit. The second move of the Holy Spirit will result in people leaving historic churches and planting new churches. In the duration of each of these moves, the people who are involved will say, "This is the great revival." But the Lord says "No, neither is this the great revival but both are steps towards it."
>
> When the new church phase is on the wane, there will be evidenced in the churches something that has

not been seen before: a coming together of those with an emphasis on the Word and those with an emphasis on the Spirit.

When the Word and the Spirit come together, there will be the biggest movement of the Holy Spirit that the nation, and indeed the world, has ever seen. It will mark the beginning of a revival that will eclipse anything that has been witnessed within these shores, even the Wesleyan and the Welsh revivals of former years. The outpouring of God's Spirit will flow over from the UK to the mainland of Europe, and from there will begin a missionary move to the ends of the earth.[1]

Even if Wigglesworth had not said that, I believe that the next thing to happen on God's calendar is not the second coming but the awakening of the church before the end. How long will this era last? I don't know.

The Lord said: "Write down the revelation . . . so that a herald may run with it. For the revelation awaits an appointed time; it speaks of the end and will not prove false. Though it linger, wait for it; it will certainly come and will not delay" (Hab. 2:2–3, NIV).

"O that Ishmael might live under your blessing!" begged Abraham, but God said Isaac would be the one. The name Isaac means "he laughs." As at Pentecost when mocking turned to fear, the Word and Spirit coming together will bring about an era when cynical laughter will turn to reverent fear and joy.

Much of the preaching I have done in my lifetime—if I am utterly candid—was Word only. When people came to Westminster Chapel, they did not expect to *see* things happen; they came to *hear* the Word. Conversely, there are churches where people go not so much to *hear* but to *see* things happen. Who can blame them?

Jesus, however, could dazzle the multitudes with the power of His word as easily as when He performed miracles. The people were astonished when He spoke and astonished when He healed. The simultaneous combination of the Word and the Spirit in great and equal measure will do that. And when this takes place, as my friend Lyndon Bowring puts it, "Those who come to see will hear, and those who come to hear will see."

PERSONAL REFLECTION

Consider the prophecy from Smith Wigglesworth. Have you seen the evidence of those church phases in your lifetime? What do you anticipate happening in the next few years?

_____

_____

_____

Spend some time with God, and ask Him what His church— fully awakened and empowered—would look like. How can you prepare your heart for what God will do through this next awakening?

_____

_____

_____

NOTES

DAY 2

1. Blue Letter Bible, s.v. "*parrēsia*," accessed December 18, 2020, https://www.blueletterbible.org//lang/lexicon/lexicon.cfm?Strongs=g3954&t=kjv.

2. Crossway, "Martyn Lloyd-Jones: 'Correct doctrine can leave the church dead; you can have dead orthodoxy, you can have a church that is perfectly orthodox but perfectly useless,'" Twitter, April 28, 2018, https://twitter.com/crossway/status/990229310144483334.

DAY 4

1. This is a typical saying used by Jack Taylor, with whom I often preach.

DAY 5

1. E. M. Bounds, *Preacher and Prayer* (Chicago: The Christian Witness Co., 1907), 45, https://archive.org/details/preacherpray00boun/page/n3/mode/2up.

2. As cited in Marva J. Dawn, *Morning by Morning* (Grand Rapids, MI: Eerdmans, 2001), 242. A variant appears on page 280 of John R. Rice's *Prayer* (Murfreesboro, TN: Sword of the Lord Publishers, 1970): "Martin Luther said that he had so much work to do for God that he could never get it done unless he prayed three hours a day!" Neither author cites a source for this saying.

DAY 6

1. Bible Hub, s.v. "*lupeó*," accessed December 18, 2020, https://biblehub.com/greek/3076.htm.

DAY 8

1. Dwight L. Moody, as quoted in *Rick Warren's Bible Study Methods: 12 Ways You Can Unlock God's Word* (Grand Rapids, MI: Zondervan, 2006), 16.

Day 12

1. Blue Letter Bible, s.v. *"prautēs,"* accessed December 23, 2020, https://www.blueletterbible.org/lang/lexicon/lexicon. cfm?Strongs=G4240&t=ESV.
2. Blue Letter Bible, s.v. *"egkrateia,"* accessed December 23, 2020, https://www.blueletterbible.org//lang/lexicon/lexicon. cfm?Strongs=g1466&t=kjv.

Day 13

1. Blue Letter Bible, s.v. *"zēloō,"* accessed December 26, 2020, https://www.blueletterbible.org//lang/lexicon/lexicon. cfm?Strongs=g2206&t=kjv.
2. Charles Carrin, "God's Remedy for Earth's 7,000 Languages," Charles Carrin Ministries, March 21, 2020, https://www. charlescarrin.com/single-post/2020/03/21/GODS-REMEDY-FOR-EARTHS-7000-LANGUAGES.

Day 14

1. Blue Letter Bible, s.v. *"sophia,"* accessed December 26, 2020, https://www.blueletterbible.org//lang/lexicon/lexicon. cfm?Strongs=g4678&t=kjv.
2. Blue Letter Bible, s.v. *"oida,"* accessed December 26, 2020, https://www.blueletterbible.org//lang/lexicon/lexicon. cfm?Strongs=g6063&t=esv.

Day 15

1. Charles Carrin, "Five Reasons Churches Have No Power," *Gentle Conquest*, April 12, 2018, https://www.openheaven. com/2018/04/12/9373/.

Day 16

1. Blue Letter Bible, s.v. *"glōssa,"* accessed December 26, 2020, https://www.blueletterbible.org/lang/lexicon/lexicon. cfm?Strongs=G1100&t=KJV.
2. Bible Hub, s.v. *"charisma,"* accessed December 26, 2020, https://biblehub.com/greek/5486.htm.

3. Jack Hayford, *The Beauty of Spiritual Language: Unveiling the Mystery of Speaking in Tongues* (Nashville: Thomas Nelson, 1996), 75–81.

Day 17

1. A. W. Tozer, *God's Pursuit of Man* (Chicago: Moody Publishers, 2015), 16.
2. Roy Jenkins, "The Welsh Revival," BBC, June 16, 2009, https://www.bbc.co.uk/religion/religions/christianity/history/welshrevival_1.shtml.
3. Lynette G. Clark, *Far Above Rubies: The Life of Bethan Lloyd-Jones* (2015; repr., Ross-shire, Scotland: Christian Focus Publications, 2016), 27–28, https://www.christianfocus.com/cmsfiles/products/samples/9781781915837_Sample.pdf.

Day 20

1. Philip Schaff, *The Creeds of Christendom*, vol. 1, *The History of the Creeds*, 6th ed. (New York: Harper and Brothers, 1877), 899, https://ccel.org/ccel/schaff/creeds1/creeds1.x.xii.html.
2. Martyn Lloyd-Jones, *Joy Unspeakable: Power and Renewal in the Holy Spirit* (Wheaton, IL: Harold Shaw, 1984), 95.
3. Lloyd-Jones, *Joy Unspeakable*, 95.
4. Charles Carrin, *Hooray and Hallelujah: Escaping Tradition and Experiencing Power* (Bedford, TX: Burkhart Books, 2019), 161–178.

Day 22

1. R. T. Kendall, *Tithing: Discover the Freedom of Biblical Giving* (Grand Rapids, MI: Zondervan, 1982), 20.
2. I learned of this from a personal conversation with someone who witnessed it firsthand.
3. I learned of this in a personal conversation and confirmed it with the preacher's staff members.

Day 26

1. As quoted in John Fowles, *The Journals*, vol. 1 (Evanston, IL: Northwestern University Press, 2003), 581.

Day 28

1. Paul Cain, "A Resurgence of the Fear of the Lord Is Coming!," Elijah List, February 13, 2018, http://www.elijahlist.com/words/display_word.html?ID=19670.

Day 29

1. Encyclopaedia Britannica, s.v. "Phillips Brooks," accessed December 29, 2020, https://www.britannica.com/biography/Phillips-Brooks.
2. Blue Letter Bible, s.v. "*chrisma*," accessed December 29, 2020, https://www.blueletterbible.org//lang/lexicon/lexicon.cfm?Strongs=g5545&t=kjv.
3. Blue Letter Bible, s.v. "*chriō*," accessed December 29, 2020, https://www.blueletterbible.org//lang/lexicon/lexicon.cfm?Strongs=G5548&t=KJV; Blue Letter Bible, s.v. "*Christos*," accessed December 29, 2020, https://www.blueletterbible.org/lang/lexicon/lexicon.cfm?Strongs=G5547&t=KJV.
4. Blue Letter Bible, s.v. "*apophthengomai*," accessed December 29, 2020, https://www.blueletterbible.org//lang/lexicon/lexicon.cfm?Strongs=G669&t=KJV.
5. Blue Letter Bible, s.v. "*chriō*."
6. D. Martyn Lloyd-Jones, *The Puritans: Their Origins and Successors* (Edinburgh: Banner of Truth Trust, 1987), 122.

Day 30

1. Charles Spurgeon, "Being the Address Delivered by C. H. Spurgeon at the College Conference, on Tuesday Morning, April 14, 1874," *The Complete Works of C. H. Spurgeon*, vol. 4, *The Sword and the Trowel* (Harrington, DE: Delmarva, 2013).

Day 31

1. James S. Stewart, *Heralds of God* (New York: Charles Scribner's, 1946), 74, https://en.wikisource.org/wiki/Page%3AHeralds_of_God.djvu/80.

DAY 34

1. Blue Letter Bible, s.v. *"analogia,"* accessed December 29, 2020, https://www.blueletterbible.org//lang/lexicon/lexicon.cfm?Strongs=g356&t=kjv.

DAY 38

1. Cain, "A Resurgence of the Fear of the Lord Is Coming!"

DAY 39

1. As quoted in David Brody and Scott Lamb, *The Faith of Donald J. Trump: A Spiritual Biography* (New York: HarperCollins, 2018), 21.

DAY 40

1. "Words for Our Time: Smith Wigglesworth—Two Distinct Moves," World Prayer Centre, accessed December 29, 2020, https://www.worldprayer.org.uk/Handlers/Download.ashx?IDMF=f3fbd2bb-0c08-4b13-a9fa-7197c54b5e6c. Smith Wigglesworth gave this prophecy in 1947.